MURPHY
MUST HAVE BEEN
A MOTHER!

MURPHY MUST HAVE BEEN A MOTHER!

(And Other Laws I Live By)

Teresa Bloomingdale

DOUBLEDAY & COMPANY, INC.
GARDEN CITY, NEW YORK
1982

Library of Congress Cataloging in Publication Data

Bloomingdale, Teresa, 1930–
  Murphy must have been a mother!

  1. Family—Nebraska—Anecdotes, facetiae, satire,
etc.   2. Children—Nebraska—Anecdotes, facetiae, satire,
etc.   3. Children—Nebraska—Biography.   I. Title.
HQ555.N2B55   306.8'7
AACR2
ISBN 0-385-17033-5
Library of Congress Catalog Card Number 82–45141

To Lee, my love,
Yesterday,
Today,
and Forever.

Contents

CONTENTS

Introduction

Trying to raise a child today is a little like trying to put a tricycle together on Christmas Eve. Few of us are trained for the job; we never seem to have the proper tools; the darn thing keeps trying to get away from us; we have a tendency to keep blaming our spouse for suggesting this ridiculous idea in the first place; and there is never enough time to do the job to our satisfaction.

Yet we persevere, and somehow, either by trial and error, or by researching the subject (which is a waste of time; the directions are always for another model), or maybe just by doing our best and trusting our own judgment, the job does get finished. Because of their parents (or maybe just to spite them), most children do grow up to be sensible, well-adjusted, even charming adults, at least until they try to put together a "trike" of their own.

For the past two decades-plus I have been working on

ten such "projects," and to my amazement, they all seem to
be turning out well. I suppose I should attribute my success as
a parent to my own parents, my husband, and my God; but
actually, I owe a lot to Mrs. Murphy.

You know Mrs. Murphy; she's the lady who wrote that
law: "If anything can go wrong, it will." (No, Mr. Murphy
did not write it; if Mr. Murphy had written it, it would have
read: "If anything can go wrong, don't try it.")

I love Mrs. Murphy's Law, for until I read it I felt that I
was the only one for whom everything seemed to go wrong.
But things go wrong for everyone, especially, it seems, those
of us who are raising children, or loving a spouse, or making
a home for a family and maybe even a career for ourselves.
For us, so much seems to go wrong!

This book is about things that go wrong for mothers. Oh,
I could write a book about things that go right, because my
children *are* good (sometimes), and my husband *is* wonderful
(most of the time), and my house *is* in order (on Christmas
and Easter, and when my mother comes to visit) and even
my career is so-so (unless you are standing in the bookshop
reading this and have already concluded you're not going to
buy it); but such a book would be so boring! (And so brief!)

No, better a book about things that go wrong, in everybody's family . . . yours, mine, maybe even our mothers'
(though I doubt that; after all, our mothers had *perfect* children). In the following pages I cover such ridiculous
"wrongs" as:

- monsters that follow little kids to kindergarten,
  and

- trips that never should be taken, and

- birthdays nobody wants, and

- grass that is spoiled rotten, and

- garbage disposals that talk back, and

- laundry that just lies there, and
- letters that were better burned, and
- costumes even Dior couldn't design, and
- people we have to put up with whether we want to or not, and
- other crazy things that happen to mothers who take on the

impossible task of raising children, or living with the same man forever, or keeping a kitchen clean, or establishing a career while simultaneously attempting all of the above.

Mrs. Murphy's right, you know. If anything can go wrong, it will.

But if nothing ever went wrong, how would we know what went right?

MURPHY
MUST HAVE BEEN
A MOTHER!

1

School Terrors

~~~~~~

"The quickest way to cure a child's stomachache is to have him stand at the front door and watch the school bus depart without him."

~~~~~~

Every autumn the nation experiences an outbreak of cowardice, as five-year-olds all across the country become terrified at the thought of their first day in school. Will I have to walk by myself? Will a monster get me along the way? Will I be able to find the school? Will the teacher let me in, or will she say: "You don't belong here; go away!"? Will the other kids make fun of me? Will I be able to find the lavatory? Will I be able to find my way back home?

Truly, that first day of school can be terrifying to a little child.

Assuming he's a boy.

Little girls have absolutely no fear of going to school for the first time. They are quite sophisticated, even about kindergarten; after all, didn't they attend the kindergarten roundup last spring, and get to meet everybody and learn all about the teacher and the classroom and the other kids?

Wasn't it fun, chatting and playing and exchanging phone numbers with the other girls, then phoning them all summer long to plan the forthcoming Great Event, SCHOOL?

True, the little boys attended the kindergarten roundup too, but they sat through the entire proceedings stoically silent, refusing to acknowledge the existence of anyone present, including themselves.

I have never been able to understand why little boys are so afraid to start kindergarten, but almost all of them are, even those little boys who have spent their preschool years being holy terrors in their own neighborhoods.

I remember one four-year-old lad in our neighborhood who was so cocky he once challenged a seven-year-old bully to a fight, and won. The victory went to his head and he then fancied himself to be the block bully, teasing and taunting everybody who got in his way, be they his peers, their parents, or his own mother.

Yet when the time came for that Holy Terror to go to kindergarten, he clung to my knees and wailed: "Don't make me go, Mama; I don't wanna go to school! Sumpun awful's gonna happen to me if I go!"

As he had spent the summer intimidating half the kids in the first and second grades, I think he may have had a point.

Since the very sight of a school bus sent the child into hysterics, his father said:

"I'll drive him to school the first day. Maybe that will make things easier for him, going off with Daddy!" And, in fact, our little son cheerfully climbed into his dad's car, waved good-bye to me and his little brothers and sister, and to my absolute astonishment, went peacefully off to school.

Twenty minutes later they were back.

"I couldn't do it," said my husband. "I just couldn't leave him there. The poor kid was terrified! I had to drag him all the way into the classroom. Even when he saw the other kids he wouldn't stop yelling. The teacher told me just to leave him, that he'd be okay. But I couldn't do that. The poor baby was scared to death!"

I looked at the "poor baby" and he looked at me, and while nary a word passed between us, he got the message.

"Give me the car keys," I said to my husband. "You stay with the little kids; I'll be right back." Come along, Terror; your hour is at hand!

We drove to the school; my son got obediently out of the car, turned back and said cheerfully: " 'Bye, Mom; thanks for the ride!"

He then went docilely into the school building, and while I drove off complimenting myself on my firmness, my Holy Terror bypassed his classroom, cased the building, snitched a cupcake from the cafeteria kitchen, locked all the lavatory stall doors from the inside, and concluded his self-guided "tour" by setting off the fire alarm.

From that day on, he loved kindergarten. (The feeling was not mutual.)

By the time his younger brother was ready for kindergarten, we had moved to a new home, one within walking distance of the school. Thus we did not have to worry about a car pool or a crowded bus. We just had to fight the battle of getting our five-year-old to walk those eight long, scary blocks.

The fact that kids in our neighborhood had been walking that route for years did not convince him of the safeness of the route. We took him on the "Walk to School" night, showing him how quiet the neighborhood was: no heavy traffic, no unleashed animals, no big bullies to tease a little kid, but it did no good: he adamantly refused to go.

Driving him was out of the question. We had only one car, which my husband took to work each morning. Walking to school with older children was also impossible; our son was in the afternoon session of kindergarten, and no older children came home for lunch. He would have to walk alone.

Only he wouldn't.

"I can't go to school!" he would cry, his big blue eyes filling up with tears. "There's a gorilla up on the corner waiting to gobble me up! You can't see him, but he's there! He hides when grown-ups come around. Do you want me to be gobbled up by a gorilla?"

By the tenth day of this, I would have preferred that he not ask me to commit myself on that point. I had done everything: bribed, pleaded, threatened, locked him out . . . only to find him at three o'clock, still sitting under the bushes next door, waiting till it was time to come home.

Then one afternoon, as he dawdled on the porch steps pleading with me not to send him to sure death, one of his little classmates came traipsing up the street, and somehow cajoled him into going to school. From that day on, our son would go to school only if Tommy told him to, and to my delight, Tommy did so, every single day for the rest of the year.

Wherever you are today, Tommy, know that you have my undying gratitude, though I do have one request. Your kindergarten pal has now been in school for eighteen years, and is still playing eeny-meeny-miney-mo with his college majors. Would you mind dropping in at Nebraska University and cajoling this kid into graduating?

The only one of our seven sons who went off to kindergarten willingly was the one we were quite sure wouldn't. Born with severe asthma, this boy had spent half his lifetime sitting on my lap, wheezing and gasping and pleading with me to help him breathe. Even after he began to receive the shots which eased his breathing, he did not want me out of his sight, so sure was he that I alone could cure his asthma. When he began to walk he would follow me from room to room, staying near me every minute of the day; if I went into the bathroom or my bedroom he would sit on the floor in the hall, with his back against the door, to be sure that I wouldn't "disappear" without his knowledge. If I left the house for a few hours, I would return to find him waiting at the window, watching for me. It was pathetic, and when he began to approach school age I became concerned that he would not be able to tolerate a whole morning away from his mother.

The situation was complicated by the fact that we had moved again, and he would have to go to a new school; none of his brothers and sisters had gone there, nor would they be riding the school bus with him.

On the first morning of school, he dressed himself silently and obediently, ate his breakfast, and clutched my hand tightly as we walked to the corner to wait for the bus.

When the bus pulled up to the curb, I anxiously leaned down to kiss my baby good-bye, and kissed empty air. The moment the bus door had opened, my "mama's boy" had bounded onto the bus without so much as a "See ya, Mom." I waved, but he didn't see me; he was too busy making new friends. He loved the bus, he loved the kids, he loved kindergarten, and he never had another asthma attack. His doctors were too kind to conclude that the kid was allergic to his mother!

My daughters, on the other hand, sailed off to kindergarten with all the aplomb of upperclassmen returning to college after a dreadfully boring summer at home. No one had to accompany, cajole, threaten, or bribe them to go to school. Going to school was what they had been waiting for and counting on for as long as they could remember. They had no qualms, no fears, no terrors . . . they were saving all that for high school.

Trying to launch a little boy into kindergarten is child's play (wherever did they get that expression? Nothing is more violent, disruptive or destructive than child's play!) compared to preparing a teenage girl for high school.

We have a daughter who started high school last fall, and I thought for a while I would have to hire a Tommy to drag her off to school.

"Aren't you excited about starting high school?" I asked her when she tossed aside a letter from her counselor.

"Oh, sure," she said, with all the enthusiasm of a convicted felon discussing Leavenworth.

"You don't sound very thrilled," I said. "Anything the matter?"

"I don't have anything to wear!" she said.

"I know that, honey," I said, "and I told you we'd go on a shopping spree next Saturday. We'll get some cute sweaters and skirts, and maybe a pair of knickers, and some new jeans. I'll even treat you to some of those alligator shirts!"

"Oh, Mother, you're really out of it!" she sighed. "If I'm going to wear the preppy knickers, I can't wear alligators! Everybody would laugh at me! Anyway, I can't buy clothes now!"

"Why not?" I asked. "School starts next week."

"I know, but I can't get clothes for school until I go to school and see what clothes I should get. What if I showed up in jeans and all the other girls were in skirts? I'd die!"

"Then wear a skirt!" I said.

"And find everybody else in jeans?" she asked. "I can't risk it!"

"Why don't you call Kathleen and ask her what she is going to wear?" I suggested.

"Are you kidding?" she asked. "She'd think I don't have a mind of my own! I think I'll just skip school the first day and spy on all the girls going into school, so I can see what everybody is wearing."

The clothes problem was finally solved when another "new girl" called our daughter, and after hemming and hawing and hinting, finally asked:

"What are you wearing to school first day?" (Brave girl!

So what if she doesn't have a mind of her own? She has courage!)

The girls finally agreed to wear blue jeans (no designer tags) and white knit shirts (no alligators), white bobby sox and topsider shoes. (And these are the girls who spent eight years complaining because they had to wear look-alike uniforms!)

"Thank heaven that's settled," said our daughter. "Now, if I can just find somebody to walk to school with . . ."

"Why not walk with Kathleen?" I asked.

"Her mother gives her a ride," she said accusingly but in vain.

"Then why not call that new girl up the street? The one who called you about clothes?" I suggested. "Ask her if she wants to walk to school with you."

"I can't do that, Mother!" she cried. "She'd think I was pushy! Anyway, if she wanted to walk to school with me she would have said something when she called me! Can we quit talking about this, Mom? You're making me nervous!"

I'm making *her* nervous!

The truth was, we were both nervous, and I could see how concerned she was about walking to school alone on that first day.

The awful morning finally arrived, and as she picked at her breakfast she admitted:

"I really thought somebody would call and ask me to walk to school with them. I guess nobody likes me."

"Do you like your friends?" I asked.

"Of course I like my friends! What's that got to do with anything?"

"You haven't called any of them to ask if they would like to walk to school with you," I said. "Maybe they are assuming that you don't like them!"

"You just don't understand, Mom," she said. "You just don't understand!"

At that moment the phone rang and a shy voice asked to speak to Herself.

"It's for you," I said, handing my daughter the phone.

"Hello," she said. "Oh, hi. Yeah, I guess so. I was supposed to meet a bunch of kids at the corner, but I'm late anyway, so I'll yell at them to go ahead and I'll wait for you. What are you wearing? Jeans? Great! See ya!"

Somehow our daughter weathered that first awful week of high school, the terrors of which only an adolescent can understand. "Who shall I eat lunch with?" ("If I sit down with a group, they'll think I'm a leech; if I sit down alone, they'll think I'm a loser!") "How friendly should I be with the teachers?" ("If I'm too friendly, they'll think I'm buttering them up; if I'm unfriendly, they'll think I'm a burnout!") "If I see a boy I know, should I speak first or should I wait till he speaks to me?" (*"Smile?* And have everybody in the whole school think I'm a flirt? Mother, you're so weird!") "I haven't got anything to wear!" ("I know, but I've already worn my jeans, and my knickers, and my overalls, and my skirts and my slacks and my kilts and my harem pants! What'll I *wear?"*)

Yes, that first week in high school can be horrible for a teenage girl, but as time goes by she will adjust and relax and even revert to her kindergarten sophistication.

I realized this the other morning when another of our daughters, a "sophisticated senior," came down to breakfast wearing Bermuda shorts.

"No school today?" I asked, as she settled herself at the breakfast table with her yogurt and diet toast.

"Sure," she said. "Why do you ask?"

"The shorts," I said. "Do the girls at Westside wear Bermuda shorts to school?"

"After today they will," she said, and breezed out the door to join three friends who were patiently waiting for her.

Every mother wants her children to be self-confident and popular and happy at school. Why, then, do I prefer the kindergartener who clings to my knees and the adolescent who cries on my shoulder?

2

The Bug and I

~~~~~~

"If she has a throbbing headache, high fever, raw throat and racking cough, it's a nuisance . . . (though he may eventually suggest she see a doctor). If he has a headache, fever, sore throat or cough, it's a crisis . . . (and she may eventually suggest that he see a lawyer)."

~~~~~~

Last week I had one of my rare battles with The Bug. Every mother is familiar with The Bug; it's that little germ that strikes once or twice a year, causing us to wake up in the morning feeling so sick we would like to die. Of course we don't get to die, or even go to the hospital; mothers get to go to the hospital only to give birth, or to tote toothbrushes, portable radios or pepperoni pizzas to members of our family who do get to go to the hospital.

No, The Bug does not make a mother sick enough to go to the hospital, but it does make her feel rotten enough to stay in bed. Though few mothers get to do that, either. Most mothers who awake with a backache, upset stomach, migraine or maybe just a horrible hangover (which I have never had but would like to try for) feel compelled to drag themselves out of bed to feed the baby, fix the family breakfast or search for the husband's socks.

But I am not that much of a martyr. When I get The Bug, I give in to it, convinced that my hour has come, if not to die, at least to sleep past 7 A.M. I don't worry too much about my illness, even though I may be throw-uppy and dizzy and too weak to walk, because while doctors claim that The Bug has no known cause or cure, both are known to me. The Bug is brought on by that "I've had it up to here!" attitude, and can be cured simply by lounging and loafing and reading a good book. No medication is necessary, though it is recommended that Mother abstain from conversation centered around whose turn it is to do the dishes and "Who told her she could wear my cashmere sweater?" and fast completely from cooking, cleaning and controversy of any kind. (Even refereeing is a no-no.)

When I was a very young mother, with two babies in diapers and two toddlers not even old enough for preschool, I never got The Bug . . . or maybe I got it and didn't recognize it. The Bug bears a striking resemblance to morning sickness (of which I had a chronic case), and when I got The Bug I always assumed it was just another case of here-we-go-again. While my husband hated to see me sick, he didn't worry too much if I woke up in the morning with The Bug, as long as I didn't wake up with it again the next morning!

I am being too hard on my husband. Actually, during those rather awful years when all ten kids were babies, toddlers or preteens, my husband was most solicitous anytime I got sick. On those dreadful mornings when I would awake nauseous, or dizzy or just out of sorts, he would insist that I stay abed while he took charge. He would dress quickly and quietly, close the nursery door so I wouldn't hear the babies wail, then herd the other children down to the kitchen where he would do what most husbands could be expected to do under the same circumstances: pick up the telephone and call Grandma.

As my mother lived one hundred and fifty miles away,

she could hardly jump in the car and come fix breakfast, but she did soothe his nerves and tell him how to drop the bread into the toaster and pour the cereal into the bowl.

I always hated getting The Bug, or any other stay-abed illness, not because my husband was so helpless, but because he wasn't. Instead of turning the whole thing over to our twelve-year-old (who was so efficient he could have single-handedly run an institution for delinquent children . . . and today often claims he did) and going to the office where he belonged, my husband would take the day off and stay home to run the household.

I remember one morning, when the kids were all small, I awoke with a sinus headache unlike any headache you have ever heard of. (*All* sinus headaches are unlike any headache you have ever heard of; just ask any sinus sufferer.) My head pounded, my ears rang, my face felt like one huge toothache and my inner ear had evidently spent the night on a merry-go-round because when I tried to walk, the bedroom floor kept waving Hello. I sank back into bed with mixed emotions. I could sure use a day loafing, but who would take care of the kids?

"Don't you worry about that!" said my husband when I moaned my bad news. "I'll take care of everything and everybody; you just get some rest." I groaned gratefully, and he went off to fight the wars. I had just sunk into a painful sleep when somebody tapped on the bedroom door.

"Mom," said my ten-year-old, "Dad wants to know where the bread is; there isn't any in the breadbox."

"Of course the bread isn't in the breadbox," I said (who could fit six loaves of daily bread in a breadbox?). "It's in the pantry, on the same shelf with the cereal." My son murmured a quick "Thanks; go back to sleep," and closed the door.

Ten minutes later there was another tap.

"Mom?" asked my eight-year-old. "Are you asleep?"

"Not now," I sighed. "Why? What is it?"

"Dad wants to know where the cereal is; he can't find anything but Poisoned Oats."

"Poisoned Oats?" I asked. "What are Poisoned Oats?"

"You know, that health cereal you bought; Dad says it tastes like dirty gravel, and he wants to know where you keep the *good* cereal."

"I don't *keep* good cereal," I said. "I buy it, but everybody eats it the same day. You might as well eat the oats, because I'm not buying anything else till they're all gone."

"Okay," he said, "but be prepared to listen to everybody rebel."

I didn't hear any rebelling, but a few minutes later I did hear another knock.

"Mother?" asked my ever-efficient daughter. "Would you please tell Dad that if he would just keep out of my way I will make eggs Benedict for everybody?"

"*You* tell him," I sighed, trying not to think of the mess she makes whenever she takes over my kitchen.

"Thank you," she said firmly. "I just wanted to be able to say you said."

My befuddled mind was still trying to decipher that when yet another child peeked into my room.

"Mama," said my four-year-old, "Daddy wants to know where you keep the pancake mix."

"Pancakes?" I asked. "I thought Mary was going to make eggs Benedict."

"Mary's in her room," she said. "She dropped all the eggs when Jim and Mike got into a fight and knocked her down."

"Why would Daddy send Mary to her room?" I asked.

"Because she picked up a gallon of milk and poured it all over Mike, then Mike couldn't see and Jim really clobbered him."

"Well, what did Dad do to Mike and Jim?" I asked. "Surely he didn't send them to their room . . . together!"

"Naw," she said. "He sent Jim outside to sweep up the glass from the window Mike fell through, and he sent Mike to the bathroom to wash off the blood."

"I think I'd better get up," I moaned, but before I could set my shivering feet on the moving floor, yet another child appeared on the scene and said:

"Mama, you're wanted on the phone. It's Grandma."

"Good morning, Mother," I said into the phone. "How are you?"

"I'm fine, dear," she said. "I just want to know where the tranquilizers are."

"The what, Mother? Did you say tranquilizers?"

"That's right," she said. "You remember those little red pills your doctor gave me the last time I came up to help you with the children; where did you put them?"

"Forgive me, Mother," I said. "I must be half asleep. But would you please tell me why you are calling at seven-thirty in the morning to ask about medicine in *my* house when you are in *your* house, one hundred and fifty miles away?"

"Oh, I didn't call you, Teresa," she said. "Lee called me. He didn't want to bother you, and he thought I might know where you keep the bandages and adhesive tape, and when I asked him why he needed them he told me, and after he told me I decided he'd better take a tranquilizer. Now, if you'll just tell me where they are, I'll tell him and he can take one and you can go back to sleep!"

Sure I can. Right after I mop up the eggs, and the broken glass, and the blood, and the Poisoned Oats (because I knew the kids would have followed their usual "If you don't want to eat 'em, spill 'em"). I dragged myself out of bed, slipped on a robe, and weaved my way down to the kitchen.

"Need some help?" I asked my husband, as I fondly

watched him trying to stuff cereal into the baby's mouth while simultaneously spreading butter on a toddler's toast.

"No," he said. "What I really need is a kiss. Do you still have The Bug?"

"I don't have The Bug," I said. "I just have a sinus headache; it's perfectly safe to kiss me."

"Safe maybe," he said, "but a waste of time."

"Well, thanks a lot!" I said. "What do you mean: a waste of time?"

"Because what I really need is a good contagious germ," he said. "After this morning, I've earned an afternoon in bed!"

As the years progressed and the kids grew older, I was able to surrender to The Bug and stay in bed with a clear conscience, knowing that the kids were able to fix their own breakfasts, and that my husband could find his own socks. My husband is a remarkable man. Born in the age of chauvinism, raised to believe that a wife's place is in the kitchen and a husband's place is at the office, he has adjusted beautifully to the modern idea of "dual roles" and "equal responsibilities," which means that he can find his own socks, if not mine. It has been interesting to watch a man who had fathered ten children but never made a peanut-butter sandwich evolve into a "person" completely at ease cooking barbecued ribs with his own special sauce, or whipping up a batch of cookies, or even doing something that takes real talent: opening a can on my long-overdue-for-replacement can opener. My husband is perfectly happy working in the kitchen, which should make my heart soar. Actually, it makes my head ache, for like many men who have achieved executive status in their profession because of their brilliant ability to organize, my husband is an absolute horror in the kitchen.

The other morning, when I awoke with The Bug, I was

too sick and sleepy to realize what I was saying when, in response to my husband's insistence that I stay abed and get some rest, I agreed to do so. Thus, when I awoke a few hours later, I dashed to the kitchen in utter panic. My worst fears were justified. My husband was "cleaning" my kitchen.

"What have you done?" I wailed as I opened the refrigerator to survey the "damage." It was worse than I feared; along with the moldy bacon and curdled cottage cheese, he had thrown out the roast beef I was sure I could get one more stew out of.

"A long-overdue cleaning job!" he said. "That's what I've done. Holy Moses, how long has it been since you cleaned those ovens?"

"Oh, lordy!" I wailed. "Don't tell me you cleaned the ovens. Now the temperature control will be all out of whack!"

"It *was* out of whack," he said. "I fixed it." Swell. Now I would have to completely readjust my own timing; I can't remember how to time an in-whack oven!

"And look how neat the pantry is!" he said proudly. "I've put all the things you use every day on the most accessible shelves."

How do you explain to a six-foot-five husband that the topmost shelves are not exactly accessible to a five-foot-two wife?

But the worst was yet to come. He had cleaned out my Thing drawer.

"I'm afraid to ask," I said. "Where did you put the stuff that was in this drawer?"

"I threw it away," he said. "It was all junk. There were broken crayons and old report cards and bent forks and Monopoly hotels and half a deck of playing cards and at least a dozen items that were completely unidentifiable, and since they've been there for months I assumed they weren't important."

"You don't understand," I said. "As long as things sit in the

Thing drawer they *are* unimportant; they may even be junk. But throw them away and suddenly you find out they are absolutely necessary to hold the house up! Prepare yourself for a disaster!"

"Actually, I'm not prepared for anything," he said, suddenly sitting down. "I feel lousy; I think I must be coming down with something."

A husband with The Bug. That *is* a disaster.

3

Sipping Is My Sport

"If God had intended for women to wear swimsuits and tennis dresses, He never would have created cellulite."

When my obstetrician announced, after the birth of my last baby, that my childbearing days were over, I was terribly depressed. Oh, I wasn't depressed because I couldn't have any more babies; few mothers of ten children find such news unwelcome. I was depressed because I knew how my friends would react to the news, and sure enough, they lived up to my expectations.

"That's terrific!" said my friend Barb when I told her that I would never again have to wear maternity clothes. "Now you can start having some fun in life! I'll sign you up for the neighborhood bowling league. We don't start playing till September; you'll be back in shape by then and ready to get away from that baby one morning a week. You'll have a wonderful time!"

While I appreciated her enthusiasm, I doubted her predictions. My experiences as a bowler were limited, but not so limited that I could not remember how inept I was at that supposed-to-be-fun sport. Personally, I could never understand why so many people think it is fun to heave a sixteen-pound ball at a bunch of pins which are much farther away than they seem and which, I am convinced, are semi-glued to the floor.

My only experience in a bowling alley (perhaps it was the name that prejudiced me; my mother always told me to stay out of alleys) was during my college days when we students used to congregate at the Forty Bowl, a combination restaurant-bar-bowling alley close to the college campus. I had absolutely no interest in bowling, but since I did have an avid interest in the opposite sex (many medical fraternities were situated in the neighborhood, and the med students also frequented the Forty Bowl), I spent many a Saturday afternoon eating hamburgers in the restaurant or surreptitiously sipping a cola in the cocktail lounge. (I was "surreptitious" for two reasons: being under age twenty-one, I was in the lounge illegally; also, I wasn't about to let those sophisticated medical students see that all I was sipping was Coca-Cola.) Occasionally I would wander into the alley side, but only to watch . . . the boys, not the bowling.

However, one afternoon I got conned into substituting for another bowler, and before the game was over, I had almost committed assault. In those days the pins were set by hand; little boys were hired to scamper up onto the pin deck after each strike or spare, return the ball, reset the pins, and scamper back down again. While they were quick, I was even quicker. I had a terrible tendency to forget those kids were there, and once my ball had been returned to me and I saw the pins were set, I would throw my ball again, scarcely giving the pin boys time to get out of the way. It made for a lively game, if not for me, then at least for the pin boys.

Frankly, I don't know what everybody got so upset

about; I rarely hit a pin boy. For that matter, I rarely hit a pin. All too often my ball would take a mysterious turn halfway down the alley and end up rolling ineffectually down the channel into the ball return. Needless to say, I was never asked to bowl again, and thus I was able to spend the rest of my Forty Bowl career doing what I did best: munching hamburgers, sipping Cokes, and flirting with the fraternity fellows.

I eventually married one of them (though he is a lawyer, not a doctor), and in the next few years I managed to avoid sports of any kind by keeping in a constant state of "expectation." Pregnancy was a perfect excuse to avoid all exercise, especially sports, which I truly do not enjoy, except as a spectator—which can be wearing enough!

So it was not until a decade or so after I had met Barb that she approached me about joining her bowling league.

"It's great fun," said Barb, unconvincingly. "We bowl every Thursday morning, and then we all go to lunch. You'll love it!"

"How about if I just meet you for lunch?" I suggested. "Really, Barb, I'm not much of a bowler. And anyway, I don't have a ball."

"You can rent one," she said. "That's probably a good idea, anyway, until you find one you are comfortable with."

Comfortable? How could anybody be comfortable hefting a sixteen-pound sphere with just three fingers!

"But I don't have any shoes," I argued.

"You can rent the shoes too," she said. "Stop giving me excuses! You're going to bowl whether you like it or not! I'll pick you up the first time, then we can work out a car pool."

I bowled, but I didn't like it. It was a bigger fiasco than the Forty Bowl.

One of the things I had forgotten about bowling was the fact that shoes are not the only attire which must be carefully considered by the bowler. While one could, in an emergency, bowl in any rubber-soled shoes, one cannot, under any circumstances, bowl in a midi-length, A-line skirt.

"Why are you wearing a skirt?" asked Barb when she picked me up. "Don't you have any pants?"

"No, I do not have any pants," I said. "I never wear pants, and neither would you if you were a size five upstairs and a size fourteen downstairs. And those statistics should also explain why I always wear A-line skirts."

"It may explain the A-line," said Barb, "but why the midi?"

"Obviously you have not seen my legs lately, Barb," I said, wincing at the thought of what ten pregnancies had done to my once-slender gams. "If I can't hide them in pants, the least I can do is cover them as much as possible with a skirt."

"Okay," said Barb, "but you may find it difficult to bowl in that outfit."

I did indeed find it difficult to bowl, but the skirt was the least of my problems. While it swirled and swung and got caught between my legs, it didn't bother me nearly so much as my bursitis. After one has spent a dozen years hefting heavy babies, dragging stubborn toddlers and swatting at speedy preteens, one's shoulder muscles are not too receptive to throwing a huge bowling ball around.

At that, I didn't do too badly. Comparatively speaking, that is. (Compared to my record at the Forty Bowl: two pins and one pin boy.) In four games, I knocked down a total of twenty-two pins. True, twenty of them were in the next alley, but that was hardly my fault. Everybody kept yelling at me to "Twist! Twist! Keep it out of the channel!" So I didn't throw it in the channel; I threw it right over it.

I lasted one whole winter on that bowling team, which, for some strange reason, decided to disband at the end of the season. It was a shame too; they had been bowling together for years. I wonder why they gave it up?

With the bowling season out of the way, I began to look forward to participating in my very most favorite summertime sport: sitting on my patio, sipping lemonade, and watching my kids beat each other at badminton. But I forgot; I wasn't going to be pregnant this summer, and would therefore have no excuse to sit the summer away, doing nothing more strenuous than keeping score.

Furthermore, my friends were not about to let me get away with all that lovely, luxurious loafing.

"You'll get fat if you sit around all summer," said my friend Jean. "Why don't you take up golf? It's a wonderful sport for women; it's not too strenuous, yet it's excellent exercise. How about it?"

"I don't have any clubs," I said, with a sense of *déjà vu*. (Didn't I go through this before on bowling?)

"I've got an extra set," she said. "My hubby gave me new clubs for Christmas; you can use my old ones."

"But I don't have any golf shoes," I argued.

"We'll get you a pair," she said. "They're on sale this week at the discount center."

"But I don't have anything to wear!" I was beginning to get desperate.

"Cut off one of those damn midis," she said, noting my below-the-knee denim skirt. "Now what do you say?"

"Jean," I said firmly, "I do not want to play golf!"

"Of course you want to play golf," she said adamantly. "Everybody wants to play golf! They just don't play because they lack self-confidence, and that's what's the matter with you, I'll bet. Come out to the club with me tomorrow morning and I'll give you a few lessons."

I think that is one of the reasons I don't like women's sports; they always take place in the morning. Personally, it's all I can do in the morning to pour the coffee, put the bread in the toaster and pick up the morning paper. I certainly could not see myself shuffling through the morning dew, waiting in line for a tee-off time, then hitting a little ball and following it up hill and down dale for the sole purpose of hitting it again. I told Jean to forget it.

Jean was willing, but my husband was not.

"Why did you turn her down?" he asked when I made the mistake of telling him of Jean's idea that I should take up golf.

"For three simple reasons," I said. "I don't know how to play golf, I don't like to play golf and I don't want to play golf."

"Don't be silly," he said. "Everybody wants to play golf." (I'll say this for golfers; they are dedicated to their sport.) "You'll love golf once you learn how to play. I'll teach you! C'mon; we'll go out right now and get you a set of ladies' clubs, some golf shoes, a cap, glove . . . and some decent clothes!"

Since I cannot say "No" to my husband (a fact which should be fairly obvious), I let him drag me to the sports center and outfit me for golf. What a mistake! Once we had spent all that money, I felt obligated to play, not just one game but the entire season.

For the first few times on the course I played golf just about like I play croquet. I stood over the ball, lined it up with my club, and SWISH . . . where did it go? Right over there; it never left the ground.

"What you need is power," said my husband. "Stop worrying so much about *where* you are going to hit the ball, and concentrate more on *how* you are going to hit it. Really whack it!"

So I really whacked it, and got fined twenty-five dollars

by the greenskeeper. (How much can it cost to replace a few little divots, anyway?)

Eventually, after much practice, I managed to hit the ball a reasonable distance if not in a reasonable direction. (My golf balls had a tendency to "turn" just as my bowling balls did.) I don't know how many balls I lost that season, but my husband tells me that I did set a unique record on the club course. According to my caddy, I hit two hundred and thirty-six balls into sand traps, one hundred and seventy-seven into the rough, nine into the club swimming pool and one into the front seat of a car passing on an adjoining highway. Amazingly, no one was injured, at least not by my golf balls. And I am sorry about the caddy, but it was his own fault for standing so close when he knew very well that I have a tendency to let go of my club in midswing.

I finally got the hang of golf and, by the second season, played a fairly good game. At least, I broke ninety. Not bad, huh? It gave me almost enough self-confidence to go on and see what I could score on the back nine.

Just about the time I got pretty fond of golf, it became a passé sport; suddenly everybody who was anybody was taking up tennis. I had never played tennis, but I was once a whiz at badminton, and it's practically the same thing, isn't it?

No, it isn't. One thing they don't tell you about tennis: the racquets weigh about one hundred and eighty pounds each. And that is when you are playing in an air-conditioned club. Outside, in ninety-eight-degree heat, they weigh half a ton.

Who ever propagated the false idea that it is *fun* to run all over a concrete court, bashing balls back and forth across a net? I'll tell you who: some babe with gorgeous gams who knows how great she looks in a tennis dress, that's who.

I am convinced that tennis is popular, not because of the

game, but because of the attire. It's the ads that grab you, not the score. You know the ads I mean: those pictures in all the elite magazines of a tall, handsome fellow in sexy white shorts, knit shirt and white sweater oh so casually thrown across his shoulders. (I'll bet it took him twenty minutes to get those arms tied around his neck like that.) In one hand he has a hand-strung racquet ("used on the best courts; only five hundred dollars plus tax"), and his other hand is resting suggestively on the shoulder of a beautiful girl, dressed in a one-piece tennis outfit designed by Dior that gives a beguiling peek at her beruffled bottom and a long look at her lovely legs.

The trouble with such an ad is: we all think we look just like them, or that we would look just like them if we only had those outfits and those racquets.

As a sensible, realistic person, I always managed to avoid such ads, until they added one factor: a tiny tinge of gray, in his hair as well as hers, plus just a few oh so becoming wrinkles around the eyes. Then I was hooked. Obviously, I had to take up tennis, since they were already running my picture in the racquet ads.

My tenure at tennis was, unfortunately, short-lived. Since I couldn't persuade my husband to play, I conned his best friend into being my partner on the club courts. We played ten minutes, but did not finish even one game because during that time period I had two telephone calls from my husband asking when would I be home, and how could we possibly be out of peanut butter; two interruptions from waterlogged sons who came running from the pool area to ask if they could get something to eat; one yelp from my daughter who came dashing onto the court to ask me if I had met the "neat new tennis pro," and yet another yell from the parking-lot attendant telling me that somebody had just driven off in my car. In all the confusion, I lost track of the score, the ball and my partner, who had given up and gone into the bar for a beer. (He was halfway through before I missed him.)

I guess I am just not a sports person. I don't even know how to swim, a fact I have always regretted, but never so much as I did this summer when our neighbors put in a pool and invited us to use it, anytime.

"The pool is beautiful," I told Shari, as she proudly showed it to me the morning it was finally finished, "and I appreciate your invitation, but I don't swim, and it's not just because I look ridiculous in a swimsuit; it's because when I get in the water I sink like a stone and stay there till somebody rescues me."

"You don't have to swim to enjoy the pool," said Shari. "Come over anyway, and we'll sit by the side of the pool and sip mint juleps. Watching the kids swim will give you a good excuse just to sit and sip!"

I think I have just found my favorite sport.

4

By Land
and by Air

"No family should attempt an auto trip if their kids outnumber the car windows."

Much has been written about the effects on people of such things as alcohol, drugs, tobacco, caffeine, and even other people, but I have never read a word about a factor which causes radical personality changes in almost every person who is exposed to it.

I am talking about travel.

What happens to people when they are "in transit"? The nicest, sweetest, sanest people seem to metamorphose the moment they find themselves on wheels, on rails or thirty thousand feet in the air.

I admit that my experience as a traveler has been very limited (though not limited enough). As a mother of ten children, I have done very little traveling because I couldn't bear to leave the kids when they were little, and I didn't dare to leave them when they got big. The only thing worse than leaving them was taking them with me.

While it may seem to some that I never take my children anyplace other than church, the hospital or traffic court, the truth is, I have taken them, many times, to visit their grandparents.

I made one grave error when I got married. I put too much distance between me and my parents. This didn't really bother my parents too much until they became grandparents. While they had seen more than enough of me, they never seemed to see enough of their grandchildren. My mother was wonderful about making the trip from St. Joseph, Missouri, to Omaha several times each year, to cuddle her darling grandbabies; but my father, busy with his job as editor of the daily newspaper in St. Joe, insisted that the mountain must come to Mohammed. And believe me, that mythical mountain's trip would have been a snap compared to mine . . . especially when the children outnumbered me, and their father found excuses to stay home.

"Why don't you take the kids and visit your parents?" he would suggest periodically; and, like an idiot, I would.

Taking our firstborn baby to see Grandma and Grandpa was a fairly simple experience, for Baby slept through the entire trip, rocked into slumberland by the gentle swaying motion of the train. But Baby did me a double cross; he turned into a toddler. And toddlers, as every mother knows, never sleep, especially when they are traveling, and certainly not if Mama wants them to sleep so that she can give more attention to the new baby.

It was after our second baby was born that I discovered the metamorphic effect of travel. Our second son, who slept like the proverbial babe when he was at home, did not share his older brother's reaction to the swaying motion of the train. He did not sleep. Instead, he threw up . . . and up . . . and up . . . and up . . . and up. This kept me a bit busy on that three-hour trip, especially since I had the toddler along too. At home, this toddler was fiercely independent, insisting that he be allowed to play on his own, alone and unsupervised. Self-reliant, self-confident, outgoing, he was mature beyond his years . . . until he heard the words "All aboard." Then he would turn into a terrified infant, crying, clinging, climbing all over me throughout the entire trip. Thus, I would have one baby shrieking in my lap and another throwing up over my shoulder, an experience that would turn the gentlest mother into a raving maniac and often did.

One would think, therefore, that I would stop taking kids on the train. But I didn't; I made that trip at least once a year, adding a new baby each year, to the consternation of the conductor, who had to keep track of them. By the fifth year I was traveling with four sons (ages one, two, three and four) and a baby daughter, who was the joy of my life because, unlike her awful brothers, she seldom cried, except when she traveled, and then she howled all the way from here to there and back again.

By this time, however, her brothers had quit clinging to me. They had become seasoned travelers, and the train was like a second home, which may explain why they were determined to destroy it. They smeared chocolate on the seats, spilled soda on the floor, drove their toy cars up and down the aisle, pestered all the passengers and left a trail of tiny toys, candy wrappers and crayons halfway across Iowa by flushing them down the train toilet because it was so much fun to watch them drop onto the tracks.

Despite the fact that the Bloomingdale toddlers terrorized the train passengers once or twice a year, there is no truth to the rumor that we caused the demise of the Burlington Zephyr. As a matter of fact, the conductor once assured me that he had heard of a family who caused even more disruption on that train than we did. I made the mistake of asking him who.

"Their name was James," he said. "Frank and Jesse."

That particular conductor was himself proof of my

theory that travel metamorphoses a person. I had ridden that train dozens of times during my college days, and that conductor had been most helpful, a gentle, kind, patient person. I noticed, however, that after I had taken my toddlers on his route five or six times, he turned into a trembling, nervous, cantankerous old codger. What a shame. But travel will do that to you, I guess.

I was sorry to see the passenger train pass into history, for truly it was the ideal way to travel with children. There was room for them to walk around; there were endless drinks of water from the fountain at each end of the car; snacks or meals were available in the diner; restrooms were large enough for a mother to change a diaper or tug on a toddler's training pants; seats were wide enough to hold a baby and a toddler too; but best of all, there was a conductor constantly on duty to scare the waddin' out of any kid who misbehaved.

With such perfect transportation, it stands to reason that they would do away with it.

Of course we still have Amtrak. But when the Amtrak people set their schedules for Omaha, they checked with the Burlington records and concluded that it might be wise to have Amtrak stop in Omaha in the middle of the night. If their idea was to discourage the Bloomingdale traveler, I've got news for them. Those "terrible toddlers" are now college-age travelers, wide awake and wildest at three o'clock in the morning.

As train travel has an effect on people's personality, so does air travel.

Have you ever watched people in an airport terminal? For the most part, they are jolly, happy creatures, excited about their prospective journey. They will stand around the gate, giving a laughing or loving farewell to those they are leaving behind, a friendly, welcoming smile to those boarding the plane with them, a cheerful greeting to the flight attendant who helps them store their carry-on luggage and find their seats. What a lively, warmhearted bunch of people!

Once in the air, they all change. Executives wipe off their smiles, put on their glasses and bury their faces in books or briefcases, where they will remain submerged until mealtime.

Teenagers who, moments before, had been whooping it up in the terminal lobby or snack bar stretch out or curl up (depending on their gender) and fall immediately to sleep.

Even those lively little children who had spent the past hour racing each other from Eastern to Braniff and back again seem to settle down in their seats, and somehow stay quiet throughout the entire trip. (I have never been able to understand this; maybe it has something to do with the air pressure. I must investigate that.)

But the greatest change occurs in mothers.

On the ground, there is no more courageous traveler than a mother. She drives car pools for kindergarteners and even cub scouts. She will sit in the death seat while her teenage son learns how to drive, and even more courageously, she will drive while her teenage son sits in the death seat, criticizing and complaining. Sometimes she will even be brave enough to drive with her husband sitting beside her. I knew one courageous mother who drove the family car for five hundred miles following her daughter, who was driving the other family car. True, the mother developed a slight facial tic, but it was only temporary.

Mothers are famous for their courage.

But put them on an airplane and they panic.

Look around you the next time you are on an airplane. You can spot the mothers every time. They are the ones holding up the airplane by clenching the armrests with their fists. They won't read a book or even glance at a magazine, because they have to keep an eye on the sky to watch for oncoming traffic. They refuse a cocktail because they know very well the plane is going to crash and they are not about to meet their Maker with liquor on their breath.

What makes a mature, self-confident, competent mother panic when she gets on a plane? Reason. Pure and simple reason. She who has spent the past week watching her ten-year-old unsuccessfully trying to fly his kite is never going to believe that a hundred tons of metal can soar safely through the air, for three hours yet, at thirty thousand feet. It's not just the aerodynamics that scare her; it's the airplane itself. Surely a machine that was invented by two brothers working *together* has got to have something wrong with it. ("Orville, did you install the aeronut?" "Why should I, Wilbur, that was your job!")

But I think the real reason mothers tend to panic on an airplane is due to the fact that there is no telephone. One cannot pull into a service station and call home to tell the kids to please check to see if the iron is unplugged, or to remind them to feed the dog, or to reemphasize your rules on at-home parties; or *to see if they're at home to answer the phone*.

That's why airports have so many telephones. Mothers can only go so long without checking on their kids.

The greatest personality changes occur not on the trains, not on the planes, but on the overland buses.

I spent four hours on an overland bus recently, and it seemed like four days because of the passengers I had to put up with. Two filthy-looking creatures, evidently bums, were sprawled across the back seat, snoring loudly.

The woman next to me mumbled and grumbled continuously about the inconvenience of traveling all this distance just to see a daughter who "probably doesn't want me, anyway; she hates it when I visit."

An obviously inebriated gent across the aisle kept weaving his way back to the restrooms, lurching into people's laps and falling over his own feet.

In the seat next to his, a timid four-year-old sat silently throughout the trip, either ill or just terrified to be sitting next to that drunk.

In the front of the bus a group of disreputably dressed young people, looking as if they had slept in their rumpled jeans and wrinkled T-shirts, twanged guitars and sang strange songs intermingled with loud laughter and unintelligible conversation. Were they runaways? Dropouts? Potheads? Who knows?

In the seat behind me a baby cried constantly, while in the seat ahead an elderly woman, probably senile, stared out the window the whole time; she was obviously unaware of the singing, laughing hippies in the front of the bus.

Weirdos, one and all. I could hardly wait to get off that bus.

We finally reached our destination, and as I watched the "weirdos" disembark, I noticed a strange phenomenon supporting my theory that travel metamorphoses people.

The "senile old lady" returned to reality simply by removing her earplugs. (She had traveled this route before.)

The "inebriated gent" once again weaved his way down the aisle, clutching the hand of the toddler who had been seated next to him, warning cheerfully: "Careful, sweetheart; it's tricky walking in this narrow aisle, even when the bus is standing still." The timid toddler, on seeing her grandmother awaiting her, leaped off the bus, shouting and waving and demanding the promised treat for "being a good girl on the bus."

The grumbling woman who had been hesitant to "impose" beamed smiles upon the lovely lady who embraced her with such obvious welcome.

The back-seat "bums" stumbled off the bus carting armloads of textbooks and discussing how much reading they must do during spring break from Harvard Law School.

So after that I shouldn't have been surprised to discover that the "hippie songsters" of the unintelligible conversations were junior members of the Lutheran Liturgical Choir from West Germany, traveling across America by bus to sing the gospel.

It just goes to show, you can't tell people by their "in-transit personalities." I know, because as I stepped off the bus, one of the choir members murmured:

"Somebody help that poor lady; she's a terrible spastic."

Of course I'm not a spastic. It's just that every time the bus lurched I had tightened my hold on the baby, grabbed for the falling toddler and turned to check on my tempestuous teenagers, which certainly would have been understandable had I not (for the first time in twenty years) been traveling alone.

5

Panic on the Podium

~~~~~~

*"If you didn't get your hair done, forgot to put
on lipstick and have a run in your stocking, you'll
be called upon to speak."*

~~~~~~

We all experience events in our life which leave us speechless.

Nothing leaves me so speechless as standing up before a
bunch of people who are expecting me to give a speech. It
makes no difference if it's a thirty-second committee report or
a thirty-minute keynote address; as soon as I step up to the
lectern and look out at that sea of faces, knowing that they
are expecting me to be witty or wise or—at the very least—
brief, my lips get dry, my palms get wet and my mind goes
blank. I am a terrified, trembling wreck. I have trained myself
to go right ahead and talk, but I have absolutely no idea what
I say, because I have never been one of those people who can
listen and talk at the same time. (You stay out of this, kids.)

I first became aware of this allergy to elocution when I
was in the seventh grade and suddenly found myself, one
awful afternoon, being called upon to give a two-minute im-
promptu talk in English class. I was frantic. The talk might as

well have been for two hours rather than two minutes; I knew it was beyond me. But I obediently approached the front of the room, turned to face my classmates and after gulping once or twice, stammering and stuttering a sentence or two, I confessed to the teacher:

"I don't know what to say."

"Say anything," she said unhelpfully. "If you can't think of something original, then tell us a story you have heard from someone else. Surely you can remember at least one story!"

As a matter of fact, that's exactly all I could remember: one story. And the only reason I remembered it was because when my uncle told it at the dinner table my mother choked on the punch line. Personally, I didn't think it was a very good story. In fact, it was really rather dumb, but it had one thing going for it: it was memorable. So I told my uncle's story, word for word, to the entire class, some of whom were even generous enough to laugh. It was funny, though; my teacher choked at the exact same point my mother had.

I thought this was such an interesting coincidence I told my parents about it at dinner that night, and immediately thereafter my father took me into his den and gently explained to me what that story was all about. I was horrified and humiliated, and swore I would never go back to school again, though of course I did, and while my reputation with the speech teacher had sunk to a low ebb, it had risen considerably with my more sophisticated classmates.

When I look back on that soul-scarring occasion, I wonder why such a corny shaggy-dog tale should be considered shocking, or even funny, or for that matter, worth telling. It certainly wasn't worth repeating, even to a bunch of bored seventh-graders.

The embarrassment soured me forever on public speaking, and I vowed I would never address an audience again, though I rather relished my new reputation and continued to tell stories in the coatroom, the cafeteria or the back row of a crowded classroom.

I kept that vow until the end of my senior year in high school when, due to circumstances which shall forever remain a mystery to me (and certainly to my classmates), I was the class valedictorian and, as such, was expected to give the valedictory address at commencement.

By this time, however, the teachers knew me well, and they had no intention of turning me loose before an audience —with a microphone yet! The valedictory address, I was told, would be written by the faculty scribe, and I was to deliver it, word for word, just as she had written it.

I agreed to memorize and recite the address verbatim (what choice did I have? They didn't give out the diplomas until *after* the address), but still it was a disaster. Oh, I didn't stutter or stammer or forget a line or even a word; the disaster was not my doing, but my classmates'. On hearing their favorite teller of silly stories spouting poetic passages and literary quotations and allegorical illusions, they broke into a fit of giggles and began to throw whispered satirical comments in my direction—unheard by the audience, as my classmates were well behind the microphone, but well heard by me.

It could have been one of my proudest moments, had I ignored the taunting, but I couldn't. I, too, began to get the giggles, and in trying to stifle them got an absolutely horrible case of hiccups. Thus, this carefully composed literary masterpiece, which was meant to be a sentimental and fond farewell to dear old Hilltop High, more closely resembled a Foster Brooks farce.

For the next few years I was too busy with college, courtship, marriage and babies to involve myself with committees or organizations that included public speaking. But when the kids started to school, I joined the PTA, and while I was seldom called upon to give a speech, I was frequently forced to stand up before the parents and teachers and give a treasurer's report, or read the minutes of the last meeting, or present a committee complaint.

As anyone who has ever stood at a lectern knows, there is nothing an audience finds more boring than a "committee report." I don't care if it's on finances, food, who's-been-smoking-in-the-lavatory, or should-we-fire-the-football-coach-for-buying- recruits- or-pretend-we-don't- know- about- it-and-win-for-a-change, nobody really wants to hear it. Especially not the fathers. Frankly, I don't think fathers should be allowed to attend PTA meetings; they put such a damper on things. From the moment they walk in the door, they want to know when they can go home, and even the promise of cookies and punch will not keep them from whispering complaints throughout the program. They murmur and mumble when the principal gets up to talk; they groan and grumble when a teacher gets up to talk; they mutter and moan when the counselor gets up to talk; and they gripe aloud if any parent gets up to talk.

"What's *she* doing up there?" a father I know will complain audibly to his wife. "How come you're not up there? For that matter, why aren't I up there? If they really want somebody who knows how to do these things right, they ought to call on me!" (Note to the nominating committee: Don't call on him. He really does not want to be on any committee, and believe me, you don't want him on any committee. At least when a woman gives a report, it's brief and simple. When a man writes a report it is fourteen pages of Whences and Thences and Whys and Wherefores, which nobody can understand, including him. Better to let him grumble from the audience than expound from the podium.)

I have given umpteen committee reports in my tenure as an active member of the PTA, and every one of them has been traumatic for me.

I remember on one occasion I had been asked to prepare a report on a proposed class project. I researched the subject, carefully composed the speech, spent hours rehearsing it and finally felt almost confident about giving it before an audience. I went to the meeting, joined the other speakers on the stage, then heard, to my horror, the speaker who preceded me give almost the exact same presentation that I had prepared. What did I do? I did what any school kid would do; I bent over, clutched my stomach and dashed off the stage . . . out to my car and home.

At another PTA meeting, I had been asked by the principal to stand up and give my thoughts on proposed changes in the school's disciplinary rules. I wasn't really too interested in the subject, as my child was within weeks of graduating, and anyway, my thoughts on school discipline have always been: if a kid needs to be disciplined, keep him after school, or make him write an extra book report, or hang him by his thumbs from the flagpole, but *don't send him home for a three-day suspension.*

However, I had great respect for that principal, and in an effort to be cooperative I agreed to her request, and dutifully stood up and gave all kinds of suggestions for changing the disciplinary procedures in the school. It was only when I was halfway through my arguments that I noticed the expression on the principal's face and realized, to my horror, that she was *anti*-change, not *pro*-change. Fortunately, I was not too convincing, and my motion for changes failed, 111–1.

While I have given dozens of committee reports, including everything from the fouled-up finances of the Cub Scout treasury to the idiotic scheduling of little league baseball games, my career as a speaker did not begin until I had established myself as a writer.

Writing is a wonderful vocation for a shy, unsophisticated person who truly likes to communicate, but only one-way. As a columnist I found I could spout off on any subject, never knowing who agrees or (more likely) disagrees, who clips the column to share with another, or who uses it to line the birdcage. I loved the idea of being able to work at home, wear what I please, and never worry about meeting the public.

What most beginner writers do not know, however, is that they will not be allowed to stay home and write. Eventually, somebody is going to drag them out on the lecture circuit, and the shy, unsophisticated writer suddenly becomes the terrified, tongue-tied talker.

Most audiences will not realize that a writer-lecturer is terrified, because when a writer becomes a lecturer he/she also becomes an actor. Nobody is a bigger bluffer than a writer who is trying to entertain an audience by the spoken, rather than the written, word. We stand at the podium (usually with our ankles crossed to offset the vertigo), interspersing our talk with seemingly confident smiles and gestures and nods, while at the same time saying silently to ourselves: "I will *not* get the hiccups; I will *not* scratch my nose; I will *not* think about the fact that my sinuses are draining and I am going to gag!" We just pretend to be suave and sophisticated and very much at ease, hoping that no one realizes that we have memorized this manuscript in front of us and, please God, don't let us lose our place!

Yes, I admit it. I always have a complete manuscript in front of me, though I seldom look at it because I am too busy following my high school speech teacher's advice to find a bright-eyed, alert listener and direct my remarks to him or her. Unfortunately, I have a tendency to focus on that droopy-lidded fellow in the front row who alternates between nodding off and looking at his watch. I know that the speech experts tell us we should never use a manuscript, only notes, but I have stopped apologizing for doing so since I discovered that many humorists do so. Like them, I seldom refer to my manuscript; it is really just a crutch; as long as I know it is there I am fine, but should it disappear I'd be all through.

I know this for a fact, because on one awful occasion my manuscript did disappear. I was to address a teachers convention one hot September afternoon, and only moments before I was to give my talk I placed my manuscript on the lectern, then turned to chat with the chairperson and two friends who had come from out of state to attend the convention. The chairperson then asked me to step to the side of the stage while she called the meeting to order and introduced me. After her very funny introduction, I cheerfully followed her at the podium, adjusted the microphone, greeted my audience and spoke the first sentence of my speech just as I reached down to adjust my manuscript . . . which wasn't there. I was dumbfounded. I continued with my memorized speech, while frantically signaling the chairperson to please return the manuscript which she had obviously picked up with her own notes. Only she hadn't. As I realized that someone, God knows who, had inadvertently removed my speech from the lectern and maybe even departed with it (which is exactly what happened; the preceding speaker, thinking it was his, snatched it up and left the building), I began to stutter and stammer and develop what every speaker dreads: a blank mind. I could not remember one more word of that carefully memorized, long-rehearsed speech.

Once again I reverted to classroom behavior, only this time I didn't have to fake an illness. I *was* sick. I apologized to my audience, explained my predicament, and walked off the stage, leaving the chairperson to pick up the pieces. The teachers were most understanding, and while I realize it had been a long and tiring day for them already, they really didn't have to applaud when the chairperson jokingly said: "Class dismissed!"

I was terribly upset by the whole thing; though I was not so concerned about losing my speech as I was about my reaction to the debacle. Why should it upset me so? No one had paid to come to hear me; everyone was obviously delighted to leave early; why did I care so much?

Because I knew that those kind, considerate teachers

would feel obligated to invite me back the following year, and they did. This meant that I would not only have to go through twelve more months of anguish anticipating another talk, but I would then have to stand up before them, like a delinquent child given a second chance, and try to make them laugh. There was only one consolation: I could use the same speech, and had a ready-made opening line.

The next year, as I once again stood facing the same teachers, I adjusted the microphone, thanked the chairperson for her introduction and launched my talk with:

"As I was saying when I was so rudely interrupted . . ."

The audience roared, and happily their laughter extended throughout my entire talk. It somehow made up for all those years of rejected PTA committee reports.

Despite the fact that I have been on the lecture circuit for several years, I still get terrified when I face an audience. Yet I keep going back for more, because I love the laughter, and the applause, and the people I meet before and afterward. I don't know if my speeches have improved any, but I have learned a few lessons about public speaking, which I cheerfully pass on to any of you who may find yourself at a lectern with a plastic smile, a tied tongue, and crossed ankles.

1. Cocktail suppers produce a better audience than communion breakfasts. If you are a humorist, stick to the dinner crowd; they'll laugh at anything after two martinis, a glass of rosé, and Kahlua ice cream.

2. Never drink more than one cocktail before giving a talk. True, the drinks may relax you, but they may also slur your speech and blur your memory, making you wonder who are all those people out there and why are they staring at you?

3. Always eat before going to give a talk at a brunch, lunch or banquet. No matter how light or lavish the fare, you are going to be too nervous to eat it. Explain this to the chairperson; otherwise, she may think you are ill and will get sick with worry that you won't live long enough to finish the program.

4. Know your audience and prepare your talk accordingly. I once accepted an invitation to speak to a ladies' luncheon, not realizing that the ladies were all over the age of seventy-five. My talk on teenagers fell on deaf ears . . . literally.

5. Find out what you should wear. After accepting an invitation to speak to a women's banquet in Iowa, I went through my closet deciding that the skirted suits, sports clothes and simple dresses would not be appropriate. So I went out and spent a small fortune on a beaded cocktail dress just for the occasion. When I got to my destination, I found that the banquet was being held in a school cafeteria, with all the women wearing skirted suits, sports clothes and simple dresses. I felt like a freak.

6. Find out about your fellow speakers. After agreeing to be on a panel at a college in Kansas, I decided to concentrate my talk on the then popular subject of "self-image," and prepared a stirring satire on those idiots who tell kids they should stand in front of a mirror for half an hour a day telling themselves how wonderful they are. I then found myself following, on the program, a popular psychologist who had several books on that very subject and concluded her speech by saying: "Tomorrow morning I want every one of you to get up, look in the mirror and say: 'Hi, you wonderful person; I love you!'" She got a standing ovation. I didn't.

6

I Can't Afford Four Eyes

"People who wear contact lenses should not have shag carpeting."

"You look like the biblical housewife searching for her lost drachma," said my husband when he found me crawling across the bathroom floor on my hands and knees, a flashlight clutched in my fist and my nose inches from the floor.

"I didn't lose anything," I said. "Dan did. I'm looking for his contact lens."

"Why doesn't Danny look for it?" asked my husband. "I want my breakfast."

"Danny cannot look for it because he can't see without it," I explained patiently. "You who do not wear glasses cannot seem to understand that those of us who do wear glasses cannot find our glasses without our glasses."

"I thought Dan had a spare pair of spectacles," said my husband.

"He does," I said with a sigh. "But he left them in his locker at school."

"That was smart," quipped my husband.

"Dan is a scholar," I said, as I felt under the sink. "Nobody ever said he was smart. In fact, very few scholars are."

"Here, let me help you," said my husband. "I'll bet I can find that lens for you." And he did. As he stepped into the bathroom we heard the tiny crunch that told us the lens had been found . . . all four hundred pieces of it.

Since this is a family-oriented book, I will not relate his subsequent remarks concerning contact lenses, irresponsible sons, and, while we were on the subject, the environmental conditions of the boys' bathroom. Suffice it to say that by eight o'clock that morning my husband had vented his spleen for the entire day. I hope his coworkers appreciated Dan's efforts on their behalf.

I must admit that I share my husband's prejudice against contact lenses. It is not just the fact that they are so expensive (actually it is, but I hate to appear pecuniary) so much as it is their losability. They are so tiny they are easy to lose sight of, and so translucent that, once lost, they are impossible to find. Furthermore, when they are lost, it is almost always in the bathroom where the loser has just showered, shaved, or brushed his teeth, splattering tiny puddles of water everywhere. And you know what a contact lens looks like, don't you? A tiny puddle of water.

I must say, however, that when it comes to searching for a contact lens I prefer the splattered bathroom to the living room (with its shag rug) or the backyard (with its deep grass) or my teenagers' bedrooms (no comment necessary).

My kids have lost half a dozen contact lenses over the years, and they almost never find them, though I must admit they are patient and persevering when they search. They learned this trait early in life.

Years ago, when our children were all little and numerous (they are now big and numerous, but there did seem to be a lot more of them when they were little), a teenage boy who was visiting across the street lost his contact lens in the neighbor's spacious and luxuriant lawn. He was sure it would be impossible to find that tiny, translucent piece of plastic in that recently sprinkled lawn, but he was determined to try, because the alternative was telling his mother that he had lost a brand-new contact lens. (Naturally it was new; nobody ever loses old lenses.)

Suddenly he had a thought. He dashed across the street, rang our doorbell, and asked to speak to all of my children.

"Oh Lord," I said. "What have they done now?" My kids were then ages eleven, ten, nine, eight, seven, five, four, three, two and one, and with the exception of the baby, they were all notorious throughout the neighborhood for their ability to aim a baseball at a picture window, or ride a bike into a parked car, or roller skate across a newly cemented yet-wet driveway.

"Your kids haven't done anything," explained the teenager hastily. "I need their help."

I called the kids together, and they listened to the teenager's tale of woe.

"Here's what I want you to do," he said. "I want you to come over to Blumkin's and line up along the edge of the lawn. Then I want you to kneel down, side by side, and crawl slowly across the lawn, running your fingers through the grass. If you find it, I'll give you five bucks. For that, you can buy out the ice cream man. Okay?"

I didn't have the heart to tell him they would have done it for free. It's only me they charge for chores.

The kids agreed to give it a try. They scurried across the street, lined up like the Notre Dame football team, and within minutes they had found the lens.

It was one of their few successful searches, and God knows they conducted many of them over the years, either looking for their own lenses or those of their friends.

Knowing all I did about contact lenses, why did I ever let my children get them?

Because of our experiences with conventional glasses.

Six of our children wear glasses, and in the years when they were willing to wear conventional framed lenses, they still managed to lose them, or leave them someplace, or bend them, or break them, usually within hours after the warranty had expired. It has not surprised me that the small optical shop where we purchased our first pair of glasses has since expanded into a multibranched, million-dollar business, most of the million coming from me.

I cannot understand why so many of our children are doomed to wear glasses. Is it because I failed to force-feed them their carrots? Or because I let them sit too close to the TV? Or is it due to the fact that they are experts at flubbing an eye exam?

I have been suspicious of my children's inability to cooperate in an eye examination ever since our son Michael was four years old and had his first eye checkup. I had taken him to the pediatrician for a complete physical, and I remained in the examining room while the doctor took Michael into the next room to read the eye chart.

"Put your right hand over your right eye," I overheard the doctor instruct Mike, "and tell me what you see on the chart."

"I see a horse and a pig and a tree and a rabbit," read Michael, obediently and correctly.

"That's very good, Michael!" said the doctor. "Now put your left hand over your left eye and tell me what you see."

"I can't see anything," said Michael. My God! My child is blind in one eye!

"Now, Michael," said the doctor patiently, "take the other hand away from your right eye *first*."

It was concluded that Michael had twenty-twenty vision; fortunately, they didn't test his IQ.

Actually, four-year-olds are about the only kids a doctor can count on to cooperate during an eye exam. Before that age, kids are too young, and after that age, they tend to joke around, or just plain lie, if not in the doctor's office, then at least in the school's annual eye test.

Eye examinations are conducted in almost every school, sometimes by the school nurse, but more often by parents who volunteer to undertake the task. The trouble with parents conducting such an exam is: parents (who wouldn't believe their own kids if they called an *A* an *A*) have complete faith in the veracity of everybody else's children. They even believe the kid who says: "I can't read any of the letters on the chart, not even the A-I-O-U-P on the top line."

Now, I don't object to school eye examinations, especially since they are free, and most especially since I have never been a volunteer examiner. What I do object to are the notes sent home ordering me to take my child to an ophthalmologist immediately and insinuating that I am a negligent mother because I haven't taken my child for regular eye checkups.

I feel about "regular" eye checkups the same way I feel about "regular" dental checkups. If the eye doctors and dentists didn't spend so much time checking healthy eyes and teeth, they would be able to fit me in when I finally reach the stage where I really can't read the telephone book, or I have a cavity that is killing me. Nothing frustrates me more than to call a doctor or dentist I have put off for three months and have him tell me he can't see me for yet another three months. You know why he can't see me? Because he's checking out some kid who conned his mother into getting him an eye appointment during algebra class.

Those notes from the amateur eye-testers used to throw me into a tizzy. I actually believed that bit about my child not being able to read the eye chart or see the blackboard, and I would immediately call the doctor for an appointment, insisting that my child could not possibly wait three months.

"If it's an emergency, of course the doctor will see her," the receptionist would say, and I would hustle my child down to the eye doctor and pay thirty-five dollars to find out that the kid has twenty-twenty vision and a yearning for Oleg Cassini glasses.

"Oh, I can't believe that," I would tell the doctor. "No girl in her right mind would want to wear glasses!"

The good doctor kindly refrained from commenting on that statement.

Why do children go through a phase where they want to wear glasses, or worse, teeth braces? Do they want to look different? Or do they want to prove to themselves that their parents are willing to spend ninety minutes sitting in a doctor's office and ninety dollars for glasses? (I won't even comment on the cost of orthodontia; I am not sure anybody loves a child that much!) Or is it perhaps, as I finally concluded, that the most popular kid in the fifth grade wears glasses (or braces) and has somehow managed to convince the rest of the kids that "this is the way to go!"

Despite the fact that I learned long ago to tell my children who want to wear glasses: "If you can't see the board, ask to sit in the front row!" and have even acquired an ophthalmologist who has eleven children of his own and can spot a liar by the second line of the eye chart, I still somehow ended up with six bespectacled children, and only a parent of a child who wears glasses can understand what this entails.

The first problem arises when you and your child go to the optician to pick out suitable frames. If you've got a boy, you're lucky; boys don't give a hoot about style; all they want is to hurry up because they have to play football at five o'clock. But if you've got a girl, you're in trouble. She will spend at least an hour trying on every pair of frames in the place, only to conclude that they are all "awful." Only when you threaten to buy her heavy-duty, guaranteed, sensible spectacles will she finally decide on the designer originals that cost twice as much, but you consent because if you stay in that store ten more minutes the optician is liable to kill the kid, unless, of course, you beat him to it.

She gets the glasses, and then comes the second problem. She wears them to school, only to come home in tears because some boy called her "four eyes," and because that popular girl who "has worn the cutest glasses ever since first grade and nobody ever called *her* 'four-eyes'!" told her, "Those frames look silly; don't you know they went out of style ages ago?" Thus, your daughter will spend the next year either refusing to wear her glasses or making every effort to get rid of them by leaving them at school, at the swimming pool, or in the middle of the driveway directly behind your back tire.

While girls are great at losing their glasses, boys are better at breaking them. I swear some spectacles are made to be broken, though, contrary to what parents sometimes believe, glasses are not made with greased screws, loose lenses, or bows that will break at the touch of a hair. Why the screws and lenses so easily fall out, or the bows so quickly break, is beyond me, but they do . . . within hours after the warranty has expired. Furthermore, I have become convinced that buying frames for glasses is somewhat like buying an original piece of sculpture; once the thing has been sold, the mold is broken. Thus, when your child breaks a hinge or a front piece or a bow, more than likely the entire frame will have to be replaced, as that style is no longer in stock, and you may also have to get new lenses because, of the thousands of frames in stock, none of them are the same shape as your lenses.

I don't know why kids are so hard on glasses. I swear my children can break a pair of glasses just by looking through them. Following are some of the excuses I have heard over the years for broken spectacles:

"I left them on the sofa and somebody sat on them."

"I put them under my pillow so I could find them in the morning."

"I was running and they just fell off."

"You told me not to wear them in the water, so I set them by the pool and somebody stepped on them."

"I was emptying the trash and they fell into the incinerator."

"I asked Patrick to put them on the porch for me, but he set them down and I mowed over them."

"I was wrestling with the dog and he bit them."

"I dunno; I just took them off and they fell apart."

"I started to kiss my girl good night and her glasses hit my glasses and they both broke."

You can see why I finally agreed to let them buy contact lenses, but it was a mistake, for while contacts are more attractive and less likely to break, they are too tiny to keep track of, and as a consequence, one or the other of my contact-wearing children is constantly losing a lens, and since they cannot see to search for them, I am the one who must crawl around the bedroom, bathroom, or backyard looking for an elusive lens.

Which is what I did again this morning. Mary was getting ready to go to work when she wailed from her bedroom:

"Mother! I dropped my contact lens and I'm late! Could you come and help me look for it?"

Sure enough, she had dropped it on her deep-pile carpeting, which meant that we both had to get down on our hands and knees to search. I prayed we would find it, because I already owed the optician a fortune for Dan's contact lens, new frames for Annie, and a conventional lens Mike broke when he was kissing that girl good night.

Fortunately, we found Mary's lens; but, unfortunately, I still had to order a new lens. Not hers, mine. While I was crawling around the bedroom my bifocals fell off and I knelt on them.

As my subsequent remarks were addressed to the Almighty, I hope He will consider them prayers.

7

Belles Lettres

~~~~~~

"Mothers who write glowing letters to their children's grandparents deserve a Pulitzer Prize for fiction."

~~~~~~

Columnist Letitia Baldrige recently wrote a requiem for the art of letter writing. It is a shame, she said, that we modernists do not take the time to relate family events or express personal emotions through letters. She claims that future generations will not only be deprived of family history, but also of those magnificent volumes of published letters which are entertaining as well as informative.

As I read Tish's comments I was reminded of that old adage of the chicken and the egg.

Will there be no more books of letters published because we modernists refuse to write letters, or do we modernists refuse to write letters because we fear they might be published?

I recently had a letter from a friend of mine in Chicago, a mother of eight children, who, over the years, has written me frequently complaining, as mothers will, of her own deficiencies as a wife, mother, and homemaker, as well as her inadequacies in such posts as president of the PTA or den mother for the Cub Scouts. Recently (to get her mind off her teenagers, I think) she got involved in politics, and to her astonishment, was considered for a presidential appointment to a very prestigious position. She wrote to me:

"If you by any chance saved my letters, please burn them. These people think I am superintelligent and sophisticated, for heaven's sake; we can't let them find out the truth!"

Unfortunately, I did not save her letters. I wish I had; I could make a mint selling them piecemeal to some tabloid.

While I, myself, do not anticipate a presidential appointment (a pardon, maybe, but not an appointment) and will undoubtedly miss my place in history, wherever it may be, I find myself pondering the Collection of Belles Lettres that would result from my past correspondence:

Dear Reverend Mother:

Thank you for presenting me with the Third Grade Spelling Prize. I am very greatful, and I will keep it allways. When I grow up I am going to be a nun like you.

Dear Miss Schwein:

Mama says I must write and apologize for my presentation in seventh-grade speech class. I don't know why. I thought it was funny. If it wasn't funny, how come all the kids laughed?

Dear Diary:

Today is my fifteenth birthday. What a bore! I only got fifteen presents from my parents. When I get to be sixteen I am going to Hollywood and become a movie star.

Dear Miss Glamour Cosmetic Club:

Please enroll me in your club. I would like to order your Rita Hayworth lipstick, your Lana Turner do-it-yourself hair-coloring set, and your Jane Russell Double-Whammy. Please send them in a plain brown wrapper.

Dear Miss Glamour Cosmetic Club:

Please cancel my membership in your club. I thought I told you to send everything in a plain brown wrapper?

Dear Diary:

Billy B. asked me to the sophomore picnic and I turned him down because he is such a drip. Then that dreamy Russ D. asked me, and Mama wouldn't let me go because I had turned down Billy B.! I got so mad I threatened to stay in my room for the rest of the year. Mama said "Fine!" and Daddy said "Promises! Promises!" All parents are drips! When I get to be a parent I am going to be perfect!

Dear Diary:

The senior prom was a dream! I went with Roger, of course, who else? We are madly in love and I get furious with my parents when they call it "puppy love." What do they know about love? There will never be anyone for me but Roger!

Dear Harvard University:

My application for admission was returned with your letter stating that you do not accept girls. May I ask why not? I find it incomprehensible that you would turn down a straight-A student just because she is female, and then accept an idiot like Roger Q. (And if anybody should know what an idiot he is, 'tis I!) Just wait, Harvard; you'll get yours!

Dearest All:

College is okay. The girls are okay. The teachers are okay. I am okay. The meals are not okay. Please send money so I can eat!

Dearest All:

Guess what, family mine? I am in love! I know you'll say eighteen is too young to be in love, but I am! His name is Jack and he is super! I can't wait for you to meet him!

P.S. Please send some more money.

Dearest All:

Sophomore year is so busy I didn't think I would even have time to date, but my roommate talked me into going to the Creighton mixer, and guess what? I met the dreamiest med student, and as soon as we looked into each other's eyes we knew we were in love! I mean, this is it! The real thing! His name is Jim, and you'll just adore him!

P.S. Jack? Jack Who?

Dearest All:

Junior year is a bummer. I hate college. I think I'll quit school and get a job. I hate school. I hate life. I feel awful, and I'm probably dying but I'm not going to any doctor. I hate doctors. Especially student doctors. Men! Do I have to finish college?

Dearest All:

You're not going to believe this, but I am going to graduate on schedule. I have a job lined up, and plan to share an apartment with Phyllis and Mary Lou. There is just one problem. The job doesn't start till July and the rent starts tomorrow. Can I borrow $100?

Dearest All:

At the risk of sending you all into a fit of hysterical laughter, I have a statement to make. I am in love. I know, I know; but this is different. In fact, we are talking about getting married. (No, Daddy, he has not actually said the magic words: "Will you marry me?" Nobody is that corny anymore.) We want a simple little wedding in church, with perhaps a prenuptial dinner the night before, and a champagne breakfast after the ceremony to get us in the mood for the afternoon reception. I think we should hold the guest list to six hundred, don't you? Naturally, I will help you with the expenses . . . just as soon as I pay my back rent and pay off the Fashion Bazaar, and get cleared with the credit bureau; I honestly don't know how those phone bills could have piled up like that!

Dearest All:

Thank you again for that wonderful wedding! The honeymoon was super, and we are finally getting settled in our apartment. Lee has turned the second bedroom into a den; it will be perfect for reading, preparing his classes, and correcting papers. Do come visit us!

Dearest All:

So much for a den. What color do you paint a room when you can't stand either pink or blue?

Dearest All:

We are moving into a house; the apartment manager says two babies are too many. Please ask Madeleine to return my maternity clothes. You asked what I want for Christmas. I want the same thing you gave us last Christmas and the Christmas before: a crib.

Dearest All:

Thanks for letting Lee, John, Mike and Jim spend the weekend with you. I know they tend to get a little obstreperous, but then you never should have told them not to climb through that attic trapdoor onto the roof. I'm sorry about the chimney. Please thank the fireman for me. Also, would you ask Betsy to send my maternity clothes the minute she is through with them?

Dearest All:

A daughter at last! And what a sweetheart she is! Why didn't you tell me about little girls?

Dearest All:

Why didn't you tell me about little girls? Gad, and I thought the boys were bad! The plumber said he can have the pipes repaired by Tuesday, and then the plasterer will fix the ceiling so the electrician can put back the chandelier. The insurance company will pay for everything but the furniture. They claim that anybody with three children in diapers can never prove those water spots came from broken plumbing.

P.S. Please ask Janet to return the maternity clothes.

Dear Teacher:

In an effort to cut down on our continuing correspondence, I have prepared the following form:

Please excuse_____(note check after one or more of the following:)

For being absent due to illness_____.

For being absent due to playing hooky

For being tardy_____.

For being late with an assignment_____.

For being cutesy in class_____.

For being not just cutesy but downright obnoxious_____.

For being_____.

Dear Sister Marion:

I must apologize for my sons' behavior at last week's basketball game between our school and yours. I admit it was improper for my kids to lead that roaring chant: "Let's beat the pants off St. Joan of Arc!" But have you thought of how your students sounded, yelling: "We're gonna clobber Christ the King"?

Dear Coach:

My son tells me that he has been on your team for fourteen games and has not yet been up to bat. I did not pay twenty-five dollars for a baseball mitt so that my boy could become a bench warmer. If he doesn't play in the next game I may have to resume my role as chief cheerleader at the junior high games. You may remember the ruckus caused the last four times I "cheered" at your games. Need I say more?

Dear Coach:

My son tells me that you have placed him on the starting lineup for Friday night's football game with Holy Angels High. Are you out of your mind? My boy is only a sophomore! Those seniors at HA will slaughter him. (They don't call them archangels for nothing!)

Dear Bureau of Traffic Violations:

What do you mean: there is a warrant out for my arrest for neglecting to pay a traffic ticket? What traffic ticket? I checked the address of the alleged parking violation and there is nothing in that block but Gloria's Go-Go Club. How could I possibly have gotten a ticket for double-parking in front of Gloria's when I have never even heard of Gloria, let alone gone to her Go-Go Club? Furthermore, the ticket is dated May 1982. I have not driven my car since 1977. Please invalidate that ticket.

Dear Bureau of Traffic Violations:

Here's your darn money, and I think that is the dumbest rule I have ever heard of. If I had known that I would be held responsible for my children's traffic violations, I would have long ago given away my car . . . or maybe even my children. Shame on you for instilling such thoughts in a mother!

Dear Harvard University:

My son's application for admission was returned with your letter stating that you cannot accept him as you have already filled your quota of straight-A male students, and are, in fact, now taking only redheaded females who speak with a lisp. I can't believe it. Just wait, Harvard; you'll get yours.

Dear Ms. Curtis:

My daughter tells me that she will need $85 for her costume as Marie Antoinette in the forthcoming school production. Couldn't she be a peasant instead?

Dear House of Dentistry:

Enclosed find $50; please apply $10 to Tim's molar repair, $15 to Patrick's cap; $10 to Peggy's crown, $12.50 to Dan's filling, and the balance to our continuing account. Please tell the doctor I love his new Cadillac. I should; I paid for it.

Dear Harvard University:

In view of the fact that you have a long waiting list, my daughter Annie is submitting her application for your freshman class four years hence. Don't bother looking for excuses. Whatever: Annie constitutes a minority.

P.S. I told you you'd get yours!

Dearest All:

How is everybody at your house? Ours is in the usual turmoil. Two crises this week: Mary has announced that she is going to leave home and get her own apartment, and John is threatening to give up his apartment and move back home. Mike never changes, except, of course, for his major. This time it's philosophy. Naturally, this means that his graduation must be postponed again. Jim wants to quit his job and go back to college; Dan wants to quit college and get a job. Peg loves being a senior in high school; she is a member of the Student Council, the Z Club, the Glee Club, the Pep Club, the Drama Club and the International Club. She says she is going to classes, but she can't remember just what they are. Ann had four by-lines in the school paper last week; the libel suits are still pending. Tim and Patrick got into a fight after dinner last night, and Tim knocked Pat through the picture window. It will cost $286 to fix the window; Pat can heal himself. Lee and Karen called and asked if I would baby-sit Joshua for the weekend, and after I agreed I remembered to ask if he still has colic. They said yes. Is it just this new generation, or have babies always cried that loudly? Sometimes I think I am too old to be a grandmother.

Dear Reverend Mother:

Remember years ago when you invited me to join your Order? Is it too late?

8

The Career Woman

"When all women become liberated, who is going to clean out the closets?"

If anybody had told me, a dozen or so years ago, that I would one day be sharing a podium with actor-author David Niven, while both of us were being wined and dined by New York publishers, and planning author tours to promote our latest books, I would have hoisted my baby onto my hip, pulled two or three toddlers out of my pan cabinet, removed a couple of teenagers from my refrigerator, and replied:

"I don't know what you've been smoking, friend, but I could sure use a puff."

For it was just a dozen years ago that I had my tenth baby, and the last thing in the world I was thinking of was a possible career, in writing or in anything else, unless maybe you consider child-harassment, which, if it is not a profession or even an art, probably should be.

Despite the fact that the Women's Movement was well underway, and housewives and even mothers were being urged to seek a career outside the home, nobody, not even the most dedicated feminist, meant to include mothers of ten children. I don't know if they considered us something special, or just beyond hope, but nevertheless, the pressure was never put upon me to go out into the world and "do something worthwhile."

Therefore, while many mothers in the early seventies were counting the days till they could seek the glamour and glory of the marketplace, I was content to go from the nursery to the nursing home, with nothing in between except kindergarten roundups, parent-teacher conferences, graduations and grandchildren. I had absolutely no desire to have any career other than motherhood, unless it was grandmotherhood; I certainly never felt any pressure put upon me to bring home a paycheck.

But alas, how was I to know that only a decade later bread would be a dollar a loaf, or blue jeans thirty dollars a pair, or that college tuition would soar to ridiculous heights and college students would take forever to graduate?

In any event, sometime amidst my contentment and my complacency inflation struck, and I finally pulled out my typewriter and made an effort to supplement the family income.

I'm lying.

When I pulled out that typewriter, I hoped to make a little money, but I had no intention of squandering it on bread or blue jeans or even college tuition. My husband could take care of those little luxuries; it was a necessity that I had in mind—namely, a cleaning lady.

Author Jean Kerr admitted that she took up writing because she liked to sleep late in the morning and society frowned on her leaving her four toddlers unfed until noon. So Jean wrote books to make money to hire a baby-sitter to feed her brood breakfast, and to keep them occupied so they wouldn't crayola the dining-room walls while their mother slept.

But I am a "morning person." I don't mind getting up with the birds, and I would much rather cook breakfast than dinner. (The menus are simpler.) As for the wall scribblings, I have long since convinced my dinner guests that that is the latest in dining-room decor. ("Cost us a fortune, my dear! The decorator is priceless!" And indeed he is that; I'll never get through paying the bills that kid has incurred.) No, my *bête noire* is not breakfast; it's housework. I hate scrubbing floors, or scouring bathrooms, or scraping gook out of my ovens. Most of all, I hate cleaning closets.

Are all closets as strange as ours? Our closets grow things. I can put a cap, jacket and scarf into a closet, close the door, and three days later open it to find a cap, jacket, scarf, two left-hand mittens and an unidentifiable galosh. By the end of the week the *ménage* has increased by two pair of roller skates, a bowling ball, three torn tennis shoes and a broken umbrella. You can only imagine what's going to be in that closet come spring.

I knew, early in my marriage, that I could never clean a closet correctly. Before we had been married six months, the two tiny closets in our honeymoon apartment were crowded to capacity. With neither an attic nor a basement in which to store our surplus, our closets became a jumble of wedding presents, sports equipment, and out-of-season clothes, most of which were my trousseau, which, for the next dozen years, were *always* out-of-season. *Any* season. Cleaning those closets, therefore, consisted of dragging everything out of the closet, whisking a dust mop around, and then frantically trying to get everything back into the closet, a feat I seldom accomplished correctly.

To complicate matters, my husband had an obsession about closet floors; he thought they should be bare, except for shoes stacked neatly on a rack. Consequently, all the boxes and cartons of presents and clothes would have to be hauled down from the shelves, then hoisted back up again, which I did dutifully until I discovered I was pregnant, and of course everyone knows an expectant mother should not be hauling or hoisting anything, and if one doesn't know that one should, or one should shut up.

So, for the next twelve years, I managed to avoid cleaning closets, as well as doing any other heavy housework, while my darling husband scrimped and saved so that I could have help. Not his, of course. Hired help. Throughout my pregnant years I had a cleaning lady who not only kept chaos out of my closets, but also cleaned the ovens, removed mold from the refrigerator, and kept my kids from killing each other. It was heaven.

It was also temporary.

Just about the time my "enceinte era" ended, the Women's Movement began, and cleaning ladies all over the country burned their dust mops, took classes in computer programming, investment counseling, or even law, and prepared to take over the country. (Which, when you realize how organized and efficient those cleaning ladies were, will certainly be an improvement.)

But the liberation of the cleaning ladies presented me with a predicament. Not only did I no longer have anyone to clean my closets, I no longer had an excuse not to clean them myself. Trim and fit and not yet forty, I was healthy as a horse, and could not for the life of me think of one good reason why I should not scour the bathtubs or scrub behind the refrigerator or clean out my closets.

So I did the only thing any bright mother would do: I created an excuse.

Though my baby was still in diapers (let's face it; my two-year-old was still in diapers, and my three-year-old was touch-and-go), I pulled out the portable typewriter that had been gathering dust since college days, bought a pack of typing paper, a dictionary and a thesaurus, and announced to my family:

"I cannot possibly clean those closets; I am too busy writing!" And in the back of my mind, of course, was the thought that I would make oodles of money that would be required to pay the high fees charged by cleaning help.

Immediately I faced the first and worst problem. I had all the necessary equipment for writing, but nothing to write about.

I had intended, in a burst of self-confidence and amateur enthusiasm, to become a political columnist. I would be sort of a Republican Mary McGrory, or perhaps a female Bill Buckley, or better yet, a combination of the two. But as I sat down to whip off a scathing editorial on the abominable state of the union, I realized that I knew little or nothing about the state of the union, except what I had read in McGrory and Buckley.

I decided to seek professional help. I would join a writers club. But I discovered that to be eligible for membership in most writers clubs, one must first be published. (And by the time I was published, I no longer had time to belong to a writers club.) I called a university professor who I knew had published many books, and asked for his advice.

"I want to be a writer," I said. "How do I go about it?"

"You sit down at the typewriter, and you write." (Which, I learned later, is all the advice any author, editor, writer or publisher will give the beginner, and it is the best advice of all.)

"But what do I write about?" I wailed. "I don't know anything but mothering!"

"So write about mothering," he said. So I did.

In the next three weeks I composed a brilliant article on

how to raise children. It was full of wisdom and knowledge and profound thoughts on parenthood. I sent it off to the *Saturday Evening Post,* and sat back to await my first Pulitzer.

What I got was my first rejection slip. Fast. Which, I discovered, is preferable to the only alternative an amateur has, which is oblivion.

Articles written by beginners go one of two routes: either they disappear into the realm of nothingness (which means you forgot to enclose a self-addressed stamped envelope), or the postman takes it out of the mailbox, drives around the block and brings it right back, with a rejection card attached. (Publishers, I have concluded, have found it expedient to supply all postmen with printed rejection slips, thus saving everybody involved a lot of time and effort.)

I soon became an expert on rejection slips. I could tell, without opening the envelope, whether this one would be a cold card signed "The Editors," a multicopied letter with a signature deliberately illegible so the writer couldn't retaliate, or possibly a nice note saying thanks but no thanks. Sometimes a manuscript was just returned, with no rejection enclosed, leading me to believe it had never been read, or perhaps the editor was just too kind to comment.

I was bemoaning the number of rejection slips I was accumulating when a friend of mine, a bookseller, free-lance writer and author, claimed that he has, in his possession, the most unique rejection ever sent out.

"Evidently this publication accepted everything," he said, "because when they rejected mine, the enclosed card read: 'We are happy to inform you that your article has been accepted for publication,' but penciled in between 'has' and 'been' was the word 'not.'"

I am sure that every writer remembers the first sale. I certainly can't forget mine, though God knows I have tried. That three-thousand-word article on how to raise children, after making the rounds of some twenty-seven magazines, finally sold. I was ecstatic!

"I did it!" I screamed as I read the letter. "Look, no returned manuscript! No rejection card! And the letter says they are buying it!"

"How much?" asked my husband, who had already invested a bundle in postage, paper and envelopes for my "career."

"Ten dollars," I admitted, as I scanned the letter.

"Just ten dollars for three thousand words?" he asked.

"It seems they aren't using all three thousand words," I said.

"How much of the article are they using?" he asked.

"One paragraph," I said with a sigh. "The one on toilet training. I wrote that I never could figure out how to toilet-train a kid, but none of ours ever wore diapers to kindergarten. They loved it! How am I going to tell my friends that my first published article was on my inexpertise in toilet training!"

While I made only ten dollars from that article, I did learn one valuable lesson from it. I could get paid for admitting my inadequacies as a mother.

Thus was born my nonsensical column on the crises, comments and crazy antics of ten children and the inadequacies of their well-meaning, if slightly demented, mother.

To my astonishment, the column was a success; within five years it had progressed from a local weekly to a national newspaper to syndication, and by the time my second book was published I was on top of the world, proud of my career, and convinced that I would someday be rich enough to hire a cleaning lady.

I was celebrating my latest literary success with friends at a country-club dinner party when I saw, seated a few tables away, my old friend, Moira.

Moira and I had gone to school together, married about the same time, and had our babies all in the same decade, though Moira had only eight, the slacker! Her husband is a hard-working but underpaid teacher, so I was surprised to note that Moira and her husband seemed to be hosting a formal dinner party for one of the town's richest and most prominent businessmen. Furthermore, Moira was wearing what had to be a Halston original, enhanced by a diamond broach and bracelet to match. I couldn't believe it.

When I met Moira in the ladies' room later in the evening I was blunt:

"Moira, what are you doing here? I didn't know you were a member of this club."

"Oh, yes," she said gaily. "We took out a membership a couple of months ago. I found it the ideal place to interview my clients."

"You're interviewing a client?" I asked. "That businessman is *your* client?"

"I haven't decided," she said. "He seems to be all right, but I haven't seen his references yet."

"His references?" I asked. "Good heavens, Moira, what on earth do you do for a living?"

"Haven't you heard?" she said with a laugh. "I'm a cleaning lady! I thought about becoming a lawyer, but this pays better."

"Just out of curiosity, Moira," I said, "do you do closets?"

"Sure," she said, "but of course that costs more."

I didn't ask her how much; if you have to ask, you can't afford it.

9

Kitchen Conversations

~~~~~~

"That mysterious piece of plastic that has been floating around your Thing drawer for the past three months can easily be identified by throwing it away."

~~~~~~

"Who are you talking to?" my husband asked me as he came out into the kitchen carrying an armload of dishes. "There's nobody here but the two of us, and I assume you weren't directing those harsh words at me! Where are the kids, anyway? Don't they know it's time to do the dishes?"

"Of course they know it," I said. "That's why they have disappeared. It is one of the unwritten rules of teendom that everything from track practice to telephone calls must be scheduled immediately after meals. Don't you remember that rule from your own youth? I certainly do. In fact, my father used to say I was the one who thought it up." (Which was absolutely untrue; it was my sister, Madeleine, who wrote that rule.)

"So if nobody's around, who were you talking to?" repeated my husband. "And what language! Shame on you!"

"You may have overheard me arguing with the refrigerator," I said, "or perhaps I was talking to the dishwasher. If I was swearing, however, it was probably directed at the garbage disposal. I can't believe my language was all that bad—you know me, I can never think of an obscenity when I need one."

"Do you often talk to your appliances?" asked my husband, as he helped me stack the dishes in the dishwasher.

"Of course," I said. "All homemakers talk to their appliances; it keeps them in shape."

"The homemakers or the appliances?" he asked.

"The appliances!" I said. "Haven't you ever heard of people talking to their plants? Well, we also talk to our appliances; we have to let them know who's boss."

"I don't like to mention this," he said, "but I think the garbage disposal is expressing insubordination; it just spit a green bean at me."

"Again?" I asked in disgust. "That's why I was speaking so harshly to it. That garbage disposal is spoiled rotten. If I feed it anything other than strained soup, ice cream or mashed potatoes, it roars and growls and puts up a real fight."

"Does it ever win?" he asked.

"Occasionally," I said, "and then it's as happy as a lark and works beautifully."

"What happens if *you* win?"

"Then it gets the sulks and refuses to eat anything at all; sometimes I have to go after it with a broom handle."

"A broom handle? You mean you beat it to death?"

"No," I said. "I beat it to life; if I force it to go around two or three times it will finally start chewing again. I hate to do that, though; sometimes, just to be mean, it will start chewing before I get the broom handle out of there. Have you ever tried to sweep with a chewed-up broom?"

"Isn't there any easier method?" asked Himself, as he

searched beneath the disposal for a reset button that should have been there but wasn't. (I always get the "other model.")

"The only other 'method' is to sack the garbage and get the kids to carry it out to the trash can," I said. "But that's hardly easier, especially if the sack breaks before the kid reaches the can, or if the kid neglects to put the lid back on, thus leaving the garbage at the mercy of the neighborhood dogs."

"Why do kids do that?" he asked. "Frankly, I would think our kids would be experts on garbage; God knows they produce enough of it. I walked by Patrick's room a while ago and saw half a sandwich, a pizza crust and half a glass of milk sitting on his desk."

"Was he eating?" I asked in surprise. "We just finished dinner!"

"Good Lord, I hope not!" said my husband. "The sandwich was curling at both ends, the pizza crust was turning green, and the milk was thick enough to spread. I'm sure the whole mess had been there for weeks! I think we should plan on sending Patrick to the University of Arizona; with his talents I'd bet he could get a scholarship."

"You lost me," I said. "What has the University of Arizona got to do with Patrick's talents?"

"Didn't you read that article in the paper last night?" asked my husband. "The University of Arizona offers a course in Garbology: the study of garbage. I'm not kidding! Patrick's perfect for that course; he's taken all the prerequisites!"

"What could they possibly teach about garbage?" I asked, incredulously.

"Oh, lots of things!" said my husband. "How to scrape it off the plates; how to sack it so it won't leak; how to carry it outside to the trash cans; how to avoid carrying it outside to the trash cans; or . . . if you have a disposal, what to say to your disposal when it gets insubordinate. There are all kinds of interesting aspects of garbage."

"I'm glad you feel that way," I said, handing him a sack. "Since the disposal isn't working and the kids are all gone, guess who gets to carry this out to the trash cans?"

"Tell me, Teresa," my husband said when I came back in the house after carrying out the garbage (there is no way I am going to explain to you why I carried out that garbage; and if you are a peace-loving housewife, I don't need to explain it), "do you talk to any of the other appliances?"

"Sure," I said, "almost every morning I have a word or two with the coffeepot."

"I hate to appear ignorant," he said, "but just what does one say to a coffeepot?"

" 'Hurry up!' " I said. "I know our coffee maker only takes three minutes, but at six o'clock in the morning, when one is waiting for that first cup of coffee, three minutes is an eternity."

"Is that the only thing you ever say to your coffeepot?" he asked.

"No," I said. "Sometimes I ask it why it looks so grungy and doesn't anybody else ever clean it but me. Other times I tell it what a good little pot it is, especially at three minutes after six in the morning, when it has brewed a particularly delicious cup of coffee. But sometimes, when the coffee is bitter, I have to threaten to call in Mrs. Olsen. That usually shapes it up; not even a coffeepot can take one more visit from Mrs. Olsen!"

"Do you talk to the dishwasher too?" asked my husband, as we stacked the last of the dishes and turned on the machine.

"Frequently," I admitted. "Especially when it leaves bits of food on the plates."

"Teresa, this machine is a dishwasher, not a disposal!

You are supposed to scrape and rinse all the food off the dishes before you put them in the dishwasher."

"I do scrape *our* food off the dishes," I said. "It's the other food I'm talking about."

"What other food?"

"The strange vegetables and sauces that show up while the machine is in midcycle. Any housewife knows about that kind of garbage. Just last night I found bits of spinach stuck to two plates!"

"What's so strange about that?"

"Nothing," I said, "except that we didn't have spinach for dinner last night. In fact, we haven't had spinach for three weeks! I don't mind washing my own garbage, but I draw the line at washing somebody else's!"

"Have you ever thought about cleaning the dishwasher?" suggested my husband.

"Why should I clean it?" I asked. "It gets cleaned three times a day!" What a dumb idea. The next thing you know he'll be suggesting that I scrub down the shower!

"I suppose you talk to the refrigerator too," said my husband, already searching for his *après*-supper snack.

"I talk to that refrigerator more than to any other appliance," I admitted. "I chastise it for luring all the leftovers to the back of the shelf so I can't see them. I scold it for putting mold on my bacon and curds on my dairy products. I yell at it for letting the kids strip it bare, and I beg it to stop leaking all over the floor every time it goes on automatic defrost. But it doesn't listen; I just may have to get tough with it."

"Before dinner it looked like you *were* getting tough with it. Didn't I see you give it a whack?"

"Oh, that wasn't because I was mad at the refrigerator," I said. "I had to give it a whack because I was so frustrated with the oven."

"Let me get this straight," he said. "When you get mad at the oven, you hit the refrigerator?"

"I didn't say I was mad at the oven," I said. "I said I was frustrated with it. The oven light keeps blinking off, and the only way I can get it to come on is to whack the refrigerator a couple of times. Your mother taught me that little trick."

"Teresa, I vaguely remember my mother whacking her refrigerator, but that was to get the refrigerator light to come on. It had nothing to do with the oven. That's ridiculous. How could whacking one appliance turn on another one?"

"I don't know," I said. "But it does. Maybe it's scare tactics. Like with the kids; whack one and the rest of them decide they'd better shape up."

"Do you think that's really fair to the refrigerator?" he asked.

"I don't believe this conversation!" I said. "How could a refrigerator know what's fair?"

"I don't believe this conversation either!" he said. "Here I am making idiotic conversation with my wife about *her* idiotic conversations with her appliances! The next thing I know, you'll be telling me that when you talk to your appliances they talk back!"

"They do!" I said, "but I'm not going to tell *you* what they say!"

Actually, I can't; their language is too awful to repeat.

10

A Broomstick, a Bent Hanger, and ?

"Show me a woman who finishes the laundry and I'll show you a woman who lives alone."

"I had a terrible nightmare last night," said my friend Mary Beth as we were stuffing envelopes for the annual Daisy Parade of Homes, a fun-type fund-raiser whereby, for a small donation, people parade through the mansions and estates of the wealthy, exulting in the magnificent furnishings, the gorgeous gardens, and the beautiful people who hostess the event. Needless to say, I never get to be a hostess; I just get to stuff envelopes.

"What was your nightmare about?" I asked Mary Beth. "Your kids?" (Does a mother have nightmares about anything else?)

"Not this time," she said. "I had an awful dream about this darn Daisy Parade."

"Why should you be uptight about the Daisy Parade?" I asked. "You're not chairpersoning any committees, and more important, your home isn't on the parade, though it certainly should be; it's lovely!"

"You're nice to say that," said Mary Beth, "but all you've seen is this living room. In fact, that's what my nightmare was about. I dreamed that my home was on the Daisy Parade, and for some reason the only way anyone could get into our house was through the laundry room. I was horrified as I watched guests climbing over and around stacks and piles of dirty blue jeans, filthy T-shirts and smelly sweat socks. And that's just what our laundry room is like, all the time! You wouldn't believe my laundry room, Teresa; I won't even let my mother go in there!"

"Your mother may not believe it," I said with a laugh, "but I certainly would. I'll put the mess in my laundry room up against yours any day. Our utility room has been filled with laundry for so long I can't remember what the floor looks like."

Personally, I think all girls should be warned about laundry before they get married. Colleges teach courses on marriage, pregnancy, childbirth, baby care and child development; they have classes in cooking, cleaning, how to handle your husband, and even how to balance your budget, but nobody ever mentions the bane of every mother's existence: the laundry. I guess they don't dare to; if they told it like it is, nobody would ever get married.

My laundry has been driving me crazy for as long as I can remember. When I was a teenager with four sisters, all of whom had the audacity to be the same size and shape as I, I was constantly losing laundry to a quicker sibling who would abscond with a favorite blouse, skirt or scarf before I could reclaim it from the laundry room.

Thus, when I got married I took great delight in knowing that what was mine would be mine and what was his would be his and it was unlikely that our laundry would become confused. It didn't become confused; what it became was a time-consuming, back-breaking burden.

"Oh, you're going to have it so easy!" my mother had told me when I got married. "That modern apartment house you are moving into has a bright, sunny laundry room, and all the machines are automatic. You won't have to spend all day Monday in your laundry room, like I did, nor will you have to spend all day Tuesday ironing. Now everything is perma-press!"

She was right about Tuesday, but she was wrong about Monday, because if one did not want to iron those perma-press clothes, one had to stay in the laundry room throughout the entire washing cycle in order to grab the clothes out of the machine before it went into spin-wring and set our perma-press clothes into perma-wrinkles.

Rather than spend all that time watching the washing machine, or worse, trying to watch the clock in my kitchen so I could dash back to the laundry room before the machine went into spin, I washed our perma-press clothes in the bath-tub, on my knees, bending over the steaming hot water, scrubbing collars and cuffs by hand and wondering just what other miracles modern science was going to impose upon me.

But the laundry really didn't defeat me until our first baby was born and I joined the diaper brigade. Abhorrent as it may seem to you modern mothers, we who had our babies "in the olden days" did not have disposable diapers. Yes, dears, we *washed* those messy things daily, or, if one lived in a small, stuffy apartment with a large, leaky baby, hourly.

When our first baby was born we still lived in that walk-up apartment where the laundry room was in the walk-down basement. This meant that several times a day I had to lug all the laundry, including the heavy diaper pail filled with soaking diapers, down to the basement where, I hoped, a machine would be available. If all the washing machines were busy, I had two choices. I could either leave the clothes in the laundry room (thus risking the wrath of my fastidious neighbors; a justifiable wrath, I must admit, for there were not only dirty diapers but also wet sheets, damp blankets, and garments our older kids later referred to as "baby's throw-up shirts"), or I could tote it all the way back up to our apartment to try again in an hour or two.

To complicate matters, the dryers took twice as long as the washers, which meant that when I finally did get a load of laundry washed, I could not necessarily get it into a dryer. So again, I had two choices: I could either hang around the laundry room to grab the first available dryer, or I could go back up to the apartment and risk having a would-be washer take my clothes out of the washing machine and toss them into the nearest corner. It took me forever to finish the day's laundry, though of course I never got the laundry actually finished, for by the time today's got done, tomorrow's was filling up the diaper pail.

Eventually we moved into a house, where glory be! I had my very own washer and dryer. True, this laundry room, too, was in the basement, but I no longer had to lug anything except the diaper pail up and down the steps, because the house had an old-fashioned clothes chute. Thus, sheets, shirts, jumpsuits, jammies, etc. could be tossed down the chute, where they would neatly land in a basket to await the hourly washing. (Yes, it was still hourly; I now had two in diapers.)

For those of you who live in modern split-level homes, perhaps I should describe the clothes chute. It is an opening in the wall through which clothes can be dropped from any floor in the house to the basement laundry room. It is a wonderful invention, most convenient if or unless you have kids. If that sentence doesn't make sense to you, let me explain.

A clothes chute is a convenience to a family with kids because there are, *ipso facto,* so many dirty clothes to be carted from bedroom to basement. But a clothes chute can be inconvenient to a family with kids, because kids have a tendency to discover that a clothes chute can be great fun for dropping things into, clothes being the last thing considered.

As my babies grew into toddlers, they began to realize the endless possibilities of that long, narrow opening in the wall, and our clothes chute became an "attractive nuisance" if not an actual danger. Many's the time I would be standing in the laundry room when I would suddenly be bombarded with toys tossed down by toddlers who "just wanted to see if they would come out in the basement." The fact that they always did come out in the basement (usually on top of their mother) did not in any way spoil their fun. They would simply dash to the basement, retrieve the toys (or what was left of them after they had smashed onto the floor or into me), run back upstairs and drop everything down again.

When my kids got older, it didn't get any better. In fact, it got worse. The tiny toys dropped into the chute were replaced by wet towels, dirty sneakers, and on more than one occasion a Coke bottle ("I wanted to see if it would break"), a tennis ball ("We wanted to see if it would bounce") and a baseball mitt ("He called me a nerd; I had to get even, didn't I?").

Even the teenagers are not without fault . . . especially if they are cleaning their rooms. Then mother can expect to be bombarded by anything and everything, from last season's clothes to the junk that was stuffed under the bed, as well as some brand-new yet-unworn jeans which have to be washed and rewashed until they are disreputable enough to be worn. Until you have been hit by, first, a soggy wet beach towel, followed by soaking sneakers, followed by three pairs of stiff new denims, you haven't lived, or maybe you were living and are no longer.

Even so, to this mother of ten children, a clothes chute was a real asset, and also a real challenge.

The challenge came when, inexplicably, our clothes

chute grew a large nail someplace between the first floor and the basement. I have never even tried to figure out how that nail got there. When you have ten children, a nail suddenly appearing in your clothes chute can be the least puzzling of your problems.

It thus became a gamble to see just what could be thrown down the clothes chute without getting caught on the nail. When something did get caught, it was either irretrievably lost, or it acted as a stopper for everything else that followed it down the chute. It was not unusual, therefore, for an entire chuteful of clothes to stack up before we realized something was caught.

When this happened we would then have to go to the laundry room and push an extra-long broomstick up the clothes chute, poking and prodding until we dislodged the clothes, then jumping quickly out of the way before we got felled by dirty laundry.

Some years later we moved out of that house into a modern split-level home with no laundry chute, but with convenient, built-in bathroom hampers.

Now, while a clothes chute is a challenge to children of all ages, a hamper is just a hamper, a simple receptacle, though not always for clothes.

To a toddler a hamper is a wonderful place to hide from your siblings or even from Daddy or Mommy. To a ten-year-old a hamper is a perfect place to put popsicle sticks, candy wrappers, or the crusts from peanut-butter sandwiches. And to a teenager a hamper is the place you stuff soaking wet towels, and more towels, and still more towels. (I can never understand why they cannot hang a wet towel on an easy-to-reach wall rack, yet can manage to stuff three of them into an already overfull hamper.)

As you might imagine, the built-in bathroom hampers at our house are always overfull, whether it be with wet towels, somebody's winter coat, or the clean clothes some kid was too lazy to put away, and this presents a real problem. The hamper is built-in immediately inside the bathroom door. All too often somebody will stuff yet one more towel into the already overstuffed hamper just as he is dashing out the bathroom door, which he always closes behind him. (It took me six kids to find out why they always close the bathroom door as they leave the bathroom; it's so I won't see what a mess they left behind.) As the overstuffed hamper slowly closes behind the quickly closing door, the crisis occurs. The hamper refuses to close all the way, thus blocking the door, which now won't open any of the way except for a tiny crack through which we can see the overflowing clothes but cannot reach them.

So we have exchanged our handy broomstick for a bent coat hanger, unwound and formed into a hook, which we must laboriously fit through the crack in the door to dig, piece by piece, enough clothes out of the hamper so it will shut fully, thus allowing the door to open.

As our kids grew into teenage and college-age, we no longer had stopped-up clothes chutes or overstuffed hampers, for each of our kids was told to do his own laundry. Thus we managed to get the chaos and confusion out of the bedrooms and bathrooms and into the laundry room, where it belongs. (Please don't tell me it doesn't belong there; I'm too old to believe those tales about neat, organized utility rooms. Those are lies; all lies.)

Surprisingly, when I announced that I had resigned as the family laundress and would, from henceforth, do none but my own and my husband's (I am liberated, but not all that liberated), our kids were most agreeable, in different degrees. Some of them willingly washed their own clothes. Others wore their clothes till they got dirty, then insisted that they had outgrown them and needed new ones. And our younger sons simply wore the same clothes even when they got too dirty or too small or both.

Oddly enough, it was the kids who washed their clothes

who caused all the chaos in the laundry room. While they were willing to do their own laundry, they were not willing to wait.

Alas, we were back to square one with the same problem I had encountered in our first apartment. While both our machines are always in use, the dryer takes longer than the washer. Thus, while one kid's clothes are drying, another kid's clothes are in the washer, wet and waiting to be dried. Along comes a third kid with his dirty clothes, and he cannot wait (have you ever known a teenager who could?), so he takes the wet clothes out of the washer, tosses them on top of the dryer, and puts his blue jeans (usually alone; he hasn't got time to gather the rest of his laundry, and anyway he's not going to wear the rest of his laundry today) into the washer. When he returns to the laundry room forty-five minutes later, he cannot put his jeans into the dryer because it is full of dry clothes, which he cannot put on top of the dryer because it is covered with wet clothes which he previously put there.

What to do? Of course, you and I both know that he could go upstairs and get a laundry basket in which to put those dry clothes, but (unless you are an eighty-five-year-old cloistered nun who can't remember the real world) you and I both know that he is not about to do this. (And a pox on you who would suggest that he cannot do this because all the laundry baskets are sitting in the upstairs hall filled with clothes his mother was supposed to sort and put away last Tuesday.)

So what does he do? He pulls the clean clothes out of the dryer onto the floor and tosses his jeans into the dryer, ignoring the priority of the wet clothes waiting on top of the dryer.

Thus we have (a) clean clothes getting dirty on the floor, (b) wet clothes getting mildewed on the dryer, and (c) a single pair of blue jeans whirling around alone at about a dollar a kilowatt. We also have one puzzled husband who can't understand why his blue sport shirt has been in the laundry since last September.

Last summer I decided I had had it. The laundry-room floor had been covered with clothes for so long I couldn't remember the pattern of the tile, the washing machine was swishing fifty gallons of hot water around one lone pair of shorts, and the dryer was going full blast with nothing in it but one small scarf.

"That does it!" I said. "I am going to put a lock on this laundry room, and from henceforth clothes can be washed by appointment only. That way I can supervise the use of the machines, and we will keep this unruly mess out of here. Do you understand?"

They understood and, to my amazement, the scheme worked. Not only did everybody's clothes get washed properly and promptly, but the stacks and piles and mountains of laundry eventually disappeared.

Unfortunately, that was not all that disappeared, and, as a consequence, another laundry crisis has arisen at our house.

This morning my husband wanted to wear his blue sport shirt, and while it is in the laundry room, clean, dry and even without mildew, I can't get at it because the laundry room is locked and I can't find the key.

Does anybody know of any household item that can be used for picking a lock?

11

How I Got Rich Washing Dishes

"If a twelve-year-old boy suggests that he has so much homework he had better get started on it right away, it must be his turn to do the dishes."

"I don't believe this!" my husband grumbled as he handed me another skillet to scour. "Why am I standing at the kitchen sink drying dishes?"

"Because the dishwasher is broken again," I told him.

"That's not what I mean!" he said. "Why aren't our kids out here doing these dishes? I am a middle-aged, overworked attorney with a briefcase full of work waiting for me in my den. So why am I out in the kitchen drying dishes? Tom would never forgive me for this!"

I had to laugh as I recalled that long-ago evening when my husband's best friend called to welcome us home from our honeymoon.

"I hope I didn't interrupt your dinner," said Tom, and my husband replied:

"No, we're finished; we're just doing the dishes."

"You're doing *what?*" asked Tom in mock horror.

"The dishes," said my husband. "I'm helping Teresa with the dishes."

"Good heaven's, man, I'm glad I called," said this happily married father of five daughters. "Evidently, no one told you of the unwritten law. We husbands do not do dishes! Put that towel down immediately before this becomes habit-forming!"

Tom needn't have worried, for while my husband continued to help with the dishes until our children were old enough to take over his tea towel, helping out never became habit-forming. In fact, he went almost twenty years without drying another dish, and for that matter, so did I. When our kids became proficient enough at pot-scrubbing, I, too, retired from kitchen cleanup, declaring my kitchen duties completed with the preparation and serving of dinner.

"You didn't answer my question," said my husband. "Why are we stuck with the dishes tonight? I thought it was Patrick's turn."

"That's why we're stuck," I said. "It seems it's always Patrick's turn, and frankly, I would rather do the dishes than redo them after Pat has done them. Just look at this skillet. I did not cook in this skillet tonight. I cooked in it Sunday night; I recognize the remains. I pulled it out of the cabinet like this; see what a "good" job Pat does?"

"Why does Pat always get stuck with kitchen duty?" asked my husband.

"It's my fault," I sighed. "I never should have told young Lee he could go study."

"What's Lee got to do with this? He hasn't lived at home since he got married five years ago, and as far as I know, he hasn't studied since he got out of college. Didn't do much then either, as I recall."

"I am referring to when he *did* live at home," I explained impatiently. "Don't you remember when Lee started high school and he had so much homework we told him that henceforth he would be excused from the dishes so he could spend that time studying? It seemed like a good idea at the time. After all, John, Mike and Jim were on KP, and by that time even Mary was old enough to help. In fact, at nine years old, Mary was the best dishwasher we had."

"Then why isn't she out here washing these dishes?" he asked, logically.

"Because she is in her room studying for her college comps," I said. "Anyway, she hasn't done dishes in years. When she went into high school, she too got out of KP, just like her older brothers before her. And why not? By that time, Dan, Peg and Annie were all helping. And when Dan went into high school, Tim took his place, as Pat later replaced Peg. For years it worked out beautifully; the older kids appreciated that extra time to study, and the younger kids, who had less homework, did the dishes. But now Patrick's the only one left in grade school, and it really doesn't seem fair that he should have to do the dishes every night, so I have been helping him out a little."

"If you are 'helping' him, then why isn't he out here helping you?" asked the attorney-for-the-plaintiff. (Do all wives feel they are constantly on the witness stand, or only those of us who are married to lawyers?)

"Patrick has a test tomorrow," I said, "so I told him he could go study with the other kids."

"If all of our offspring are so busy studying," said Himself somewhat sarcastically, "then why is 'M*A*S*H' blaring from the family-room TV? And why are both of our telephones busy? And why is your car just pulling out of the driveway? I think we've been had. The time has come to pass some new laws in this household."

The next night at dinner, he announced: "There have been some changes made on the kitchen-duty roster; your mother's name has been removed and everybody else's reinstated. From now on, each of you, regardless of age or school status, will take your turn doing dishes. I don't care if you work alone or in pairs, make up your own schedule; just see that the dishes are done, and don't expect your mother to help."

For the next few days things worked out very well. Dan and Mary did the dishes that night, Peg and Ann took the next night, Tim and Pat got Friday night.

Then came Saturday night . . . Mary and Dan's turn again.

"I can't do the dishes tonight," said Mary. "I've got a date. Dan, if you do them alone tonight, I'll let you off next time it's our turn."

"I can't do them tonight either," said Dan. "I've got a meeting at school. We'll trade with Peg and Ann."

Peg and Ann were delighted to oblige; Saturday-night supper is simple compared to Sunday dinner. But the next day, neither Mary nor Dan showed up for Sunday dinner, so Tim and Pat traded their Monday for Sunday. But Monday night Mary had to go to play practice and Dan had to judge a speech contest, and since both Peg and Ann had early baby-sitting jobs, Tim and Pat got stuck again.

By Tuesday night the schedule was so mixed up I had no idea whose turn it was, but I knew whose turn it wasn't, and that was Patrick's. But after dinner, as his older siblings quickly dispersed in different directions, Patrick cheerfully began to clear the table.

"Wait a minute, Pat," I said. "It's not your turn. You've done the dishes the past two nights. I would think you'd be upset with your brothers and sisters, sticking you with the dishes all the time."

"Oh, I don't mind," said Pat, as he scurried out to the kitchen with an armload of plates.

"Come back here," said his father. Pat came back for another load of dishes, and his father continued:

"Pat, I can understand how the kids might shaft you with

the dishes, but I will never believe that you don't mind. What's the deal? And where's your partner Tim?"

"Tim wasn't interested, so the deal's all mine," said Pat happily. "Half a buck each; that's the deal! That means I make a buck every time I take Mary and Dan's turn on KP. 'Course I can't get that much out of Peg and Annie, 'cause they don't have much money, so I give them a special deal: a quarter each, and they do my history homework. I can't wait for Jim and Mike to come home; they *hate* to do dishes!"

"It sounds like you made a good deal, Pat," said his father. "If you keep doing the dishes by yourself, you may get rich."

"And *you* may get ptomaine," I said as I handed my husband a tea towel. "C'mon; maybe Pat will give us a percentage if we do the pots and pans."

Which explains why we may be the only parents in America who get paid for washing our own dishes.

There used to be a saying that once a kid got old enough to help around the house, he was no longer around the house to help. This did not refer so much to teenagers, who are certainly old enough to help (though nobody has ever proved it, because no teenager has ever tried it), as to young adult offspring who once felt compelled to leave home the moment they reached their majority. They would rather pay half their wages for a cold-water flat complete with cockroaches than continue to submit to the "unreasonable requests" of their parents, like: "Please don't use the shower at four o'clock in the morning, or the telephone either," though a frequently ringing phone is certainly preferable to her perpetual presence. (Doesn't that girl have a home of her own?)

However, with the high cost of rent, utilities, insurance and groceries (actually, it's the shampoo that breaks them), young adults are now opting to live at home long after college. Our children are no exception. While our older sons have been away to college, and one in the Marine Corps, it is not unusual for one or more of them to move back home periodically, to remain a few weeks or a few months or at least until their creditors have lost track of them. For the parents of such yo-yos (so called because they move out and they come back and they move out and they come back) I have nothing but praise and prayers. But for you young adults between the ages of twenty-one and whatever, I offer here a few pointers on how to survive in a houseful of parents.

1. If you are not going to be home for dinner, please inform your mother of that fact before 3 P.M. If you are going to be home, notify her anyway. It is not that she wants to keep track of you; she just wants to keep track of the roast.

2. If you are going out in the evening, it is expected that you make your parents aware of that fact (if only so that they won't search the entire house yelling, "Jim! You're wanted on the phone," only to find out you aren't home). You are also expected to let your mother know at approximately what time you will be home. This will prevent her from calling the police when she wakes up at 3 A.M. and finds your bed empty.

3. For those of you who are crazy enough to smoke, please do not put out your cigarettes in (a) the bathroom basin, (b) your dinner plate, (c) your bedspread, (d) the beer can your father just set down for a moment while he went to answer the phone. While smoking is discouraged, smoking of anything other than tobacco is *verboten!*

4. While it is true that we once told you that your friends are always welcome in our home, we did not expect the word "always" to be taken quite so literally. From henceforth, therefore, your girlfriends (whatever your "relationship") must be escorted to their own homes before 1 A.M. and will not be welcomed back before breakfast. It is also requested

that your old college chums or former Marine buddies who drop in to say "Hi" limit their visits to two weeks or less.

5. Anyone who stays out all night will be assumed to have moved out. (Sorry; at 7 A.M. your little brother moved into your bedroom.)

6. Everybody who lives in this house is expected to contribute to the upkeep of this house, whether it be painting, doing minor repairs, or helping with the dinner dishes. (It should be noted that traditional male-female roles have long since been abolished. Being male is no longer a reason for refusing to run the vacuum cleaner.) For those of you who are so busy working at your jobs, or continuing your education, or just keeping up with a fast-paced social life, that you do not have time to fulfill your household responsibilities, there is a solution. It is called "money." Be prepared to part with it.

12

Forty IS
a Very Good Year

~~~~~~

*"If your family and friends insist on celebrating
your birthday, you're forty."*

~~~~~~

Nothing in the history of recorded time has been so maligned
as the fortieth birthday. Nobody wants it; everybody dreads
it; many ignore it; even more lie about it. (Which explains
why 53 percent of the population is thirty-nine years old.)

Forty is the one birthday we would like to forget, and it's
the one all our friends insist on remembering, with practical
jokes or clever parties all insinuating that "this is it, pal;
you've had it; you're over the hill."

In my opinion that's the best part of turning forty: being
"over the hill." For mothers especially, the hill can be pretty
steep, and she breathes a big sigh of relief on reaching the
peak, with only the downhill slide ahead of her.

There are a lot of bad birthdays, but forty isn't one of
them.

Thirteen, however, is.

Thirteen is a terrible time in a person's life. At thirteen, you are not a little kid anymore, yet you are not yet welcome into the exciting world of the teenager. You have to pay adult prices everywhere, but nobody would dream of treating you like an adult.

Thirteen is old enough to be assigned such teenage chores as mowing the lawn or cleaning out the gutters or waxing the kitchen floor, but come Friday night and you want to go to the Teen Disco or the post-football-game party, guess who's still too "young"?

Thirteen is an awful age for a girl, because unlike her older sister who claims she doesn't have anything to wear but really does, thirteen really doesn't. She may have a closet full of clothes, but none of them fit. They are either too small, because she has grown two inches since Saturday, or too big, because her mother insisted that she "buy a larger size so you can grow into it," which must have put a hex on her because she immediately stopped growing.

Thirteen is also a terrible age for a boy, if for no other reason that that he has suddenly become aware of the girl he has been sitting next to since first grade. However, he dare not acknowledge this awareness, for the simplest request to borrow a pencil, or even a "Hi" in the hallway, will be interpreted by his peers as a declaration of "love" and he will then have to spend the rest of the semester swearing he "hates her; she's a dog!"—a statement that will leave her puzzled and hurt, especially since she has just recently decided, after seven years of detesting *him,* that he is really rather neat.

No, thirteen is not a very good year.

Nor is sixteen.

Sixteen is even worse than thirteen, because nobody has any illusions about thirteen, while sixteen is supposed to be the magic age. Every kid wants to be sixteen, so he can drive, and date, and earn some real money working at a part-time job. Wow, man, sixteen is where it's at!

Except that sixteen comes, and it isn't there after all.

You get a driver's license but seldom get a chance to drive, because an older sibling always seems to have first dibs on the car. The part-time job takes up all your free time, which leaves little or no time for dating, and if perchance that miracle occurs when you get a night off and the car as well, sure enough the light of your life is already booked.

Sixteen is even worse for a girl. Having spent the past year counting the days till you can finally date, the magic birthday comes and goes but the telephone still doesn't ring. Your brothers try to tell you that guys don't call you because they are busy working or can't get the car, but you know the truth: boys don't call you because you are ugly and clumsy or because you got a better grade than they did in advanced algebra or driver ed. And a lot of good *that* did you; your driving privileges are restricted to running errands for your mother or toting your little brother to ball games, and would somebody please explain to you why it's okay for you to chauffeur half the seventh grade home at ten o'clock at night but you can't drive around with your friends at that same hour?

Sixteen may be all right for rich boys and gorgeous girls, but for most kids it's just another year of battling intolerant teachers and intolerable parents. The only good thing about sixteen is the fact that it lasts only twelve months (though it seems like twelve years), and then you get to be seventeen.

Seventeen is the ultimate, glorious age. As a high school senior you suddenly become sophisticated, self-confident, and on top of the world. You are the best, the brightest, the greatest . . . the graduate! Enjoy seventeen, for it, too, lasts only twelve months (though it seems like twelve days), and then you must turn eighteen.

Eighteen is a bummer. Like thirteen, it's a limbo. You can no longer live like a teenager, yet neither are you an adult. With high school behind you and college underway, you think you are too old to be living at home, but your parents think you're too young to be out on your own. Actually, home wouldn't be so bad if it just wasn't inhabited with older siblings who have more privileges than you do or younger siblings who have fewer responsibilities than you do or parents who seem to be particularly prejudiced against people eighteen. They keep harping on you to register to vote (or worse, for the draft) and to "stay out of bars; you're not an adult yet, you know!" They make boring statements starting with "When I was your age . . . ," never realizing that that was a hundred years ago and things are different now. They want you to go to college but not to the college you want to go to, and insist that you earn your own spending money and then have a fit if you spend it. They make stupid suggestions like: "Get in at a reasonable hour" and "Get up for your eight o'clock class"; and ask such ridiculous questions as: "What does his father do?" and "What do you mean, you have a 'meaningful relationship'?" Parents are a real pain in the neck when you are eighteen, but bear with them; they'll change a lot in the next few years.

A lot of people think the twenty-ninth birthday is the worst, because it's too close to thirty, which they consider the end of their youth (rather than forty, which they consider the end of everything). I'm afraid I cannot give you a personal appraisal of twenty-nine because, frankly, I remember very little about twenty-nine. I do remember that I was pregnant that year (not hard to remember; I was pregnant *every* year!) and I had four sons under the age of five, which may explain why God has mercifully erased that era from my memory.

Unfortunately, there are records to recall various events of my twenty-ninth year, like the medical files at Children's Hospital, which show that the Bloomingdale boys made eleven visits in as many months to have their stomachs pumped for ingested aspirin, ink, nose drops, sand, soap, laxatives, liquor and an assortment of other unknown products.

The accounting records of a local glazier show that the Bloomingdales paid, that year, for no less than nine broken windows, two cracked mirrors, one storm door, and the panel covering the fire alarm at the Duchesne preschool. (There was no charge for the fire call.)

The files of various insurance companies show claims for one broken arm (he fell out of a tree), one crumpled fender (he ran into it while riding his tricycle, which was not even scratched; General Motors take heed), one dining-room ceiling (he flooded the bathroom again), and one front porch (the four-year-old firebug strikes again).

The only disappointment I had on turning thirty was the discovery that I was not yet too old to have babies (five more in fact), which should explain why I concluded that forty should be a very good year.

I can understand why some people may hate being forty, but certainly no mother dreads that birthday. For forty means so many things:

- The babies have all been born, and may be already in school!

- The career you planned in college can finally come full flower.

- The home you have always wanted has been found and bought and settled into if not paid for, but at least there'll be no more moving!

- The gray hair and wrinkles so feared and dreaded came when you were too busy to care, and are now gone again, because you have time for coloring and cosmetics (you didn't look that good at thirty!).

- The worries—underdone meals, overdue bills, temperamental in-laws, terrible report cards, screaming kids, broken bicycles, tearful teen-agers—are all still very much in evidence; but by this time, who notices?

- The parents: ah, the best part of forty must be the fact that finally you appreciate your parents. You realize that they are, and have always been, wise and wonderful, loyal and loving, good and true, perfect parents; perfect people! They deserve the good times they are having in the autumn of their years: the trip to Europe, the Caribbean cruise, the retirement cottage by the sea, or even just the chance to be alone to-gether, at last, surrounded by peace and seren-ity.

Forty? Who wants to be forty? I want to be sixty-five!

13

The Green Grass of Home

~~~~~~

"Of course the grass is greener on the other side of the fence. Why do you think the neighbors put up the fence?"

~~~~~~

When I was a little girl my father used to come home on a summer's afternoon and tease me because I had been doing "nothing more tedious than watching the grass grow."

If Daddy were around today, he would be surprised to see that I am still "watching the grass grow," and I have never undertaken a more tedious task. When one has as much invested in grass as I do, one dare not take one's eyes off it, even for a minute, lest it curl up and pout because of imagined neglect. Our grass is spoiled rotten, let me tell you.

It was my spouse who did the spoiling, not I. From the first thaw of spring to the first frost of fall, all my husband wants to talk about is grass, grass, grass. Why isn't it growing? Why is it growing so fast? Why is it so pale? So patchy? So parched? Does it need water? More fertilizer? More food? And the worst catastrophe of all: *Who walked on that grass?*

We spend more time, money and effort raising our grass than we do raising our kids.

In these days of luxury lawn care it is hard to believe that for thousands of years grass just grew, all by itself. What happened? Why did lawns decide they deserve such sophisticated care? I think they must have gotten uppity when we changed their names. When I was a kid the only "lawn" in town was the Forest Lawn cemetery. Live people just had yards. And it never occurred to anybody that yards should be fed preemergents, or poked with little holes so they could breathe, or power-raked, power-mowed, or power-sowed. The only thing we did to our grass was cut it when it got too high, water it when it got too dry, and acknowledge our appreciation of it by sitting on it, rolling in it, or running across it as we played hide-and-seek, kick-the-can, tag or croquet.

I only knew one family who fertilized their grass, a rich family down the street whom nobody could stand, not because they were snobbish but because they were "smellish." The fertilizer they used to cover their yard was straight from the barnyard. (To this day I cannot understand why it was so expensive. I have been in barnyards, and believe me, there is plenty of that stuff for everybody.)

But sometime during that era everybody began reading John Marquand novels, and realized that the patch of grass surrounding their house was not a yard but a lawn, and should be treated accordingly.

And I do mean treated . . . and treated . . . and treated. Taking care of a lawn can become an obsession, and nobody is more obsessed with his lawn than my spouse.

On the first sunny Saturday in spring, he rushes outside with clipboard in hand, noting what, where and when to power-rake, aerate, feed, fertilize, spray, sprinkle, mow and manicure. He searches for embryonic webworms and would-be weeds, planning their extermination before they even exist.

Of course, he does not actually perform any of the above-named chores; he simply notes when, where, and how they should be done, as well as by whom. Fortunately, I am not the "whom." (Why do you think we had all these kids?) Our children are assigned the various tasks; all I have to do is find the children, then hound them until they complete the chores, which they usually do willingly enough if I first: lug the lawn mower to the repair shop and back; go get the gasoline, oil and new sparkplug; find the sprinklers we bought last spring and lost last fall; replace the hose which would be in perfect shape if Mary hadn't just driven over it and squashed the nozzle; find the wrench to fix the faucet so it won't squirt all over the side of the house; sneak into the neighbor's garage to retrieve the rakes we loaned them last season and they never returned; go to the nursery to buy fertilizer, preemergent and seed; put the wheel back on the spreader which somehow jumped in front of my car when I drove into the garage, and pace off the yard to pick up possible projectiles which nobody ever seems to see but me.

Once the lawn has been raked, aerated, fertilized and fed, my real job starts. I must watch the grass grow, and decide when it needs to be mowed, weeded, or watered.

Unfortunately, we do not have underground sprinklers. Consequently, I must decide when and where the sprinklers are to be set. Until I got married I didn't realize just how much talent this takes. I have yet to get it right.

"Why haven't the sprinklers been going today?" my husband will ask on a warm summer's eve, and I will have to admit that I forgot because I was involved in something frivolous like cleaning the basement or taking one of the kids to the allergy clinic.

On the days I do remember to set the sprinklers, Himself will come home and shout: "What idiot watered the lawn? We just fertilized it!"

Speaking of sprinklers, those of you who do not have underground sprinklers may be interested in my extensive experience along those lines.

When purchasing a sprinkler, I discovered that the salesman will always recommend the "traveling" model. He recommends this for one reason: it's the most expensive. I bought a traveling sprinkler one year and I'll say this for it: it traveled. I set it at eight o'clock in the morning, and by nine-thirty it had wandered across the driveway, through the neighbor's tulip bed, and out into the street. I never did get the thing to follow a straight line.

The following year I bought an "adjustable" sprinkler. This allegedly adjusted for lawns of varying sizes, from a tiny patch of grass to an acre or so. There is only one problem with an adjustable sprinkler. If you have a tiny patch of grass, it invariably gets stuck on "acre" and waters the street, the neighbor's car, and the neighbor's baby sunning in his carriage. If you have an acre, the sprinkler will spray a radius of six feet and stop. I have never been able to figure out how my sprinkler knows when to readjust itself, but it does know. How else could it so accurately aim at our driveway the moment my husband comes home in his newly washed car?

I have never had an underground sprinkler, but my neighbor does, and she swears it is just as erratic as my cheap-o model. She claims that no matter how carefully she sets the timer, the sprinkler system turns on faithfully during a rainstorm, in the middle of a lawn party, and the moment her mother-in-law walks across the yard.

After much experience, I have found the perfect sprinkler. It's expensive, but it's permanent, and if it should get too old to work, it can (in my case, anyway) be easily replaced. It's called a teenage son. I just set him on the porch with a hose in one hand and a can of soda in the other, and after only one or two lessons he will learn to hit the grass and not the girl sunbathing next door.

Contrary to what my kids claim, keeping the grass mowed is no big deal in these days of power mowers. What *is* a problem is keeping track of the mower. Now, it is not easy to misplace a lawn mower, but our kids do, every summer.

(They have a special talent along those lines. They once misplaced their grandmother . . . and I refuse to believe their story that she "packed up and ran away." Though God knows, I wouldn't blame her.) Someplace in this neighborhood there must be a cache of lawn mowers and garden tools which my kids have left, loaned out, or just lost.

The only real problem involved in mowing the grass is how much to cut and how much to leave.

"Dad says he wants the grass two inches high," my son will complain. "What am I supposed to do, carry around a ruler?" He claims that no matter how conscientious he is, he can't win.

"Raise the mower!" his father will order. "You are scalping the lawn!" So the kid raises the mower, works like a slave for four hours, only to have his father come home and ask: "When are you going to cut the grass?"

There is also a problem of what to do with the grass that is cut. Most modern mowers have grass-catchers. Theoretically, they are a great idea, but practically, they seldom work. We have had four grass-catchers. One spit grass, one leaked grass, one shoved grass back into the mower motor, and the fourth, which proved to be the best, followed his brother around the yard raking.

As for the problem of weeds, our kids solved that early on. They figured out that if they mow frequently, their father won't be able to recognize the difference between the weed stumps and the grass. For we have all learned that, despite his compulsion to have a lovely lawn, he will settle for any ground cover that looks green.

If my husband is obsessed with growing grass, he is fanatical when it comes to overgrown shrubs.

"Those have to go!" he will announce with a sweeping wave toward a thicket of pfitzers that look like they have been in our yard since the third day of Creation. And I wince, because I know what the removal of such ancient evergreens entails.

First I must help him find the power saw, which is not, as he claims with total confidence, in the basement workshop in the carton marked "power saw." (For some reason, that carton holds Christmas ornaments.) It seems the power saw is not in the basement at all, nor is it on the back porch, or in the garage, or under Patrick's bed. (Those of you who have twelve-year-old sons can understand how it could have been under Patrick's bed.)

Where do power saws go? Did we take it to be repaired and leave it at the shop? No. Could we have left it in the trunk of the car? No. Loaned it to the neighbors and forgot to retrieve it? (Had we borrowed it from the neighbors in the first place, along with the rakes? Good Lord, those are *their* rakes! I must sneak them back somehow.)

Alas, the power saw is not to be found, so we must buy a new one, plus a special cord that it requires, plus a converter so that the special cord will plug into our unspecial outlet.

Then I must find the kid assigned to cut the pfitzers; he wandered off while we were searching for the saw. Once found, he will then want to argue about the estimated worth of the work he is about to do. (Our kids don't do anything they don't get paid for, except drive my car, which they will do for free providing I pay for the gas.) I also am expected to stand beside him and offer comfort and consolation as he hacks and cuts and grumbles and growls about how "this stuff is petrified; it's like cutting concrete!"

Once the branches have been cut away, the roots must be removed. Nothing takes root so firmly as a pfitzer. My son claims he had to dig all the way to Kansas to find the end of the roots, and those seemed to be permanently attached to Oklahoma.

The last time we took out a bunch of pfitzers I went

through four sons and one automobile transmission before I was through. Nevertheless, it was a fascinating experience because of the treasures we uncovered: a baseball, a mitt, three golf balls, my sterling silver gravy ladle (which has been missing since the youngest child outgrew the sandbox), and . . . you guessed it . . . the long-lost power saw.

I must admit that, once the shrubs have been removed or pruned to a more attractive shape, and the grass cut and manicured, our yard is lovely enough to be called a lawn. So I was not surprised when I came home the other afternoon and found my son sitting on the patio, gazing proudly at the vast expanse of beautiful bluegrass.

"Nothing more tedious to do than watch the grass grow?" I teased.

"That's exactly what I am doing," he said.

"You are watching the grass grow?" I asked incredulously.

"That's right," he said. "I figured that if a watched pot never boils, watched grass won't grow so fast either."

14

Who Is the Patient?

"To find an instant cure for your ailing husband . . . put him in the hospital."

A "patient," according to the dictionary, is "one who is willing to put up with waiting, pain, trouble, etc., enduring calmly without complaining or losing self-control."

How, then, did such an eponym ever get tagged onto a person who is tossing and turning on a hard-as-a-board hospital bed, muttering threats and curses and swearing that if he ever gets out of this blankety-blank place he will burn it down, because the blankety-blank nurses won't bring him a pain pill, a cigarette, or even a blankety-blank bedpan!

As anyone who has ever been in a hospital knows, there is no one less patient than a patient, especially a patient who is recuperating and expects to be dismissed this afternoon but just found out that his doctor went out of town for a long weekend and won't be back till Tuesday. (One of my fondest memories is of a doctor friend of mine who, having been hospitalized for minor surgery, was getting ready to go home when the desk refused to dismiss him because *his* doctor had left the hospital without signing the dismissal orders. The hospital shook with that doctor's shouts, or perhaps the shaking was due to the laughter of his fellow patients, who thoroughly enjoyed his predicament.)

From the moment an ill or injured person enters the hospital, he or she is expected to "be patient!"

I get hysterical when I recall those old Dr. Kildare shows where the ambulance speeds up to the emergency entrance, and before the paramedics have even opened the ambulance doors, six doctors and three nurses come dashing from the hospital to assist the suffering soul therein.

As anybody who has ever been through such an experience knows, that is not the way it goes.

In real life, the ambulance or car bringing the emergency case more than likely cannot even get into the emergency entrance driveway, because some jerk has left his car there. And in the unlikely event that you can pull up to the entrance, nobody comes to your assistance except maybe a security guard, and all he is interested in is whether or not you qualify as an emergency and thus have the right to be there.

If you are passed by the security guard, you still have to get past the insurance clerk.

"Wait a minute!" she will call, as you crawl bleeding across the carpet. "You can't go back there! You have to fill out the forms first!"

"All right," you gasp, "just show me where to sign."

"You'll have to take a seat and wait your turn," she will say, and it does no good to claim that you are bleeding from both ears, have a terrible pain in your chest, and are sure that both your legs are broken; you still have to wait your turn.

So you sit down next to a little kid with a cut finger and a teenager who fell down while playing football, and try to take your mind off your pain by reading one of the exciting magazines provided by the medical staff (*The Yachting*

Quarterly, How to Double That First Million, The Malprac-
tice Monthly and *Reader's Digest,* January 1973).

Just about the time the bleeding stops, the pain abates
and the symptoms disappear, the clerk will call your name
and you will have to answer a zillion questions, beginning
with: "How do you plan to pay?"

"By death benefits," I answered one time, and the clerk
dutifully typed my response before asking: "Is that with a
group?"

I must admit that most of my hospital stays have been in
the maternity wing, the one department where they do *not*
keep you waiting, especially if this is your tenth visit.

The last time I walked through that maternity entrance
as a patient, the security guard himself hustled me right
through to the elevator, calling to the clerk at the reception
desk:

"Forget the paperwork unless you want problems!" (The
"problem" being Patrick, who was determined to be born immediately, if not sooner.)

As we waited impatiently for the elevator (where *do* ele-
vators go?) two doctors strolled up to the elevator, took one
look at me huddled over, my arms embracing my "condition,"
and said:

"We'll walk up." ·

The cowards.

Incidentally, I made it to the delivery room, timed perfectly, as I had planned, to bypass the labor room and all the
uncomfortable (and, I have always been sure, unnecessary)
preparations enforced therein. The doctors don't like it if the
patient is wheeled into the delivery room wearing a cocktail
dress and spike-heeled slippers, but when you are about to
give birth to your tenth baby, the last thing you are concerned
about is what the doctors don't like.

Patients in the maternity wing are seldom impatient, because none of them are really sick and all of them are in a

jolly mood, except maybe for the middle-aged woman in bed three who gave birth to twins the day after her youngest child entered high school. But we in the maternity wing had no need of pain pills or bedpans, and the only time we rang for a nurse was when we needed a fourth for bridge or more ice for the lemonade. We were not even impatient to be dismissed; who is eager to trade in breakfast-in-bed and afternoon naps for cooking, cleaning and middle-of-the-night feedings? No, most of my hospital stays were a pleasure, an insurance-paid vacation, though there is no truth to the rumor that I had the last five babies just to get a few days' respite from the first five.

On a couple of occasions, however, I was incarcerated (there is no better word for it) in the hospital for surgery, and if ever a patient's patience is tested, it is while anticipating, or recovering from, surgery. Surprising as it may seem to those of you who have never gone "under the knife" (or worse, under the nose cone), the anticipation is often worse than the recovery. This is due to the fact that you are given too long a time to anticipate.

I have never understood surgeons who say: "Well, it looks like there is something there; I'm not sure just what it is, or how serious it is, but it will have to come out. I'll set you up for surgery three weeks from Wednesday."

This gives you almost a month to imagine yourself into an advanced stage of terminal whatever, and while the "something" may very well turn out to be a simple cyst, you are not yet cured; you still have to be treated for high blood pressure, tension, a facial tic and the continuous trembling of all ten fingers. When the surgeon knows you are going to have to undergo a frightening operation, why can't he set it up for tomorrow, or better yet, this afternoon?

The only operation they set up for the very next day are the ones you would rather postpone for a week or two, like your child's tonsillectomy. Invariably, when a child has to have surgery, the doctor doesn't even give the mother time to buy decent pajamas, for heaven's sake, let alone wash behind his ears. (As any mother of an eight-year-old knows, this task takes at least three days.)

Before almost every operation the patient is given a sedative several hours before being taken down to surgery. Ostensibly, this is to make you sleepy, thus hastening the effects of the anesthetic. But in fact, that Mickey Finn is supposed to knock you out so that you won't be aware of what goes on in pre-op.

The last time I had surgery, my little pill didn't work, and I was wide awake and alert when I was wheeled downstairs (by two teenage aides who were competing in the national hospital-cart demolition derby), where I was left, lying on my cart, clothed only in a sheet, in the corridor outside the operating rooms. In the next ten minutes I witnessed the following:

1. A surgeon bounding out of an operating room shouting: "Some idiot sent in the wrong X-rays; I damned near took out the wrong lung!"

2. A nurse, crying in the corridor that she was "going to picket this place until they get some decent equipment! Who can work with machines that keep shorting out?"

3. My own surgeon, who wandered down the corridor, patted me on the head and said: "Don't worry about a thing, pal; we'll have that appendix of yours out in no time," which somehow failed to comfort me, since I was scheduled for surgery on my shoulder.

The recovery room is almost as frightening as pre-op. While you are still woozy from the anesthetic, nurses and aides loom over you like vaporous monsters shouting:

"Wake up! Wake up! Come on now, wake up!" when all you want to do is sleep, or:

"Cough for me, sweetie; let's see how hard you can cough!" when all you can utter is "uuuhhh," and even that tears your insides out.

Then there is the awful thirst. Since they have deliberately desalivated you for the anesthetic, you wake up with your tongue glued to your teeth and the inside of your mouth feeling like it is lined with cotton batting. You beg and beg for a drink of water, and the only thing worse than being denied one is being given one, which, after you have swallowed it, comes right back up along with about a gallon of bile.

As you are still disoriented from the anesthetic, you are not sure just exactly where you are, and somehow you become convinced that you must still be back in pre-op, because if the surgery were over, you would, of course, be dead. (Nobody in their wildest dreams believes that they will survive surgery.)

Eventually you get oriented, and that too is terrible because nobody will believe that you are oriented; and when you say things like "For God's sake tell my husband to go home and turn off the spaghetti, I left the sauce boiling!" everybody just laughs and says, "Isn't she funny?" Yeah, funny; they can just scour that damn pan!

Eventually they wheel you back up to your room, where you become convinced that you have been left to die, because everybody has obviously deserted you. For the next three days the only time you will see a nurse is in the middle of the night, when she wakes you up to ask you if you would like a sleeping pill. They tell you that you can "ring for the nurse" any time you need something, but as every hospital patient knows, that little bell does not alert anyone. It merely sets off a recording which says: "Can I help you?" and after a pause: "I'll send someone right in."

Much has been written about the fact that nurses never seem to respond to that bedside buzzer, but in fairness to the nurses, I must admit that I tend to take their side. On more than one occasion I have been standing at a hospital desk when that buzzer sounded. The last time I deliberately listened in, and in a forty-five-second time period the same patient buzzed five times: once with a request for a Seven-Up, once with a request for more ice, once with a request for a back rub, once with a request that the redheaded nurse be sent in to give the back rub, and once to ask why nobody was paying attention to his requests.

If the tag "patient" should be hung on anybody in the hospital, it probably should be the nurses.

Or better yet, the spouse of the patient.

As much as I hate being sick, undergoing surgery, or finding myself, for whatever reason, confined in the hospital, I would choose that any day over having my husband confined therein.

Why is it that when a wife is in the hospital, her husband considers himself an absolute saint if he shows up once a day for a fifteen-minute visit, but when the husband is in the hospital, he expects the wife to come by every hour on the hour, or better yet, stay there around the clock?

My husband claims that if he is hospitalized he wants me at his bedside at all times not because he expects twenty-four-hour service, but because he wants somebody to be sure "those idiots don't kill me." This fear stems from his certainty that all medical personnel who undergo the wrath and rages of the patients are in a unique position to wreak their revenge, and given enough incentive, probably will.

There is no question, however, about the fact that my husband, like most, wants some very special attention when he is sick. Men are like children in that respect, which is only fair, I suppose, because when children get sick they tend to act like men!

Nothing gives a little kid more self-confidence than being hospitalized. Once he realizes that a mere moan or groan will bring instant attention, while the mere punch of that buzzer brings unlimited ice cream, he becomes as assured and bossy as the most demanding executive.

He also becomes a smart-mouth.

I went to the hospital one morning to visit our nine-year-old son, who was recovering from a painful though uncomplicated knee injury. While I was there, the doctor made his rounds, which, in our son's case at least, consisted only of a glance at the knee, a pat on the leg and a hearty: "You're doing fine, lad; I'll see you tomorrow!"

Whereupon our son replied: "You mean that's it? That's all you're going to do? Just look at my leg and leave?"

"That's it for today!" said the doctor with a smile.

"And for that I suppose you're gonna charge five dollars!" said our son. "What a ripoff!" To my relief, the doctor laughed (though he and I both knew that visit cost fifteen dollars!).

Children truly can be trying patients; they hate the pain, they don't understand the treatment, they are afraid of the hospital and everybody in it. But that's not when they are trying. They are trying when they are well on the road to recovery and become so bored they keep pestering the doctors, nurses, aides, janitors and anybody else who wanders past their room to bring them something to eat, or to play with, or to please change the television channel, or to "just come in and talk to me a minute."

Yet, surprisingly, most medical personnel prefer pediatrics to any other wing in the hospital. Busy doctors linger to listen to yet one more ridiculous riddle; exhausted nurses will take extra time to calm a fear or answer a question; medical technologists make a game out of giving a shot or taking blood; aides cheerfully cart ice cream and comic books and crayons and games; the cleaning help, who ordinarily wouldn't say a word to a "regular" patient, will combine mopping duties with spinning a fantastic tale to an enthralled little listener; and even that "recorder" who answers the buzzer shows more care and concern when the one demanding attention is a child.

If there are any "patients" in hospitals, surely they are the people who work in pediatrics.

15

Dere Santclos . . .

~~~~~~

"If you want a white Christmas, don't let Santa bring your child a sled."

~~~~~~

While letter writing may becoming a lost art, writing letters to Santa Claus is still a popular pastime, especially in the primary grades where teachers are frantically trying to keep six-, seven- and eight-year-olds occupied during that last hectic week before Christmas.

Following are a few examples of the creativity and confidence (not to mention greed) of a group of third-graders who were assigned Letters to Santa Claus as a class project. Fortunately, I was able to rescue these gems before the conscientious teacher had time to correct them and send them off to the North Pole. (Of course, she would send them on to Santa Claus! Teachers are Believers, you know. They have to be!)

Dear Sanna Clas,
    For Christmas I want a tenspeid bike and a raesing set and a gun that shoots real water. Pleese hurry.

Love, Martin

Dear Santa Claus,
    I hope you have a very nice Christmas. I hope I have a very nice Christmas. By-by.

Love, Julie

Dear Santa,
    How are you doing? I am doing good. Will you get me skies and boxin gluvs and candy and toys and if I thing of enything else I'll let you no.

Love Patty.

Dear Santa,
    My mommy says I can have a doll that eats and drinks and cries but duznt know how to wet.

Love, Annie

Dear Santa,
    Plese bring me a baby bruthr for Chrismas. My dad says you dont have babees at the North Pole and maybe you will bring me a puppy insted. Id rather have a baby bruthr. P.S. You can bring a puppy to if you want to.

Luv, Tim

Dear Santa,

Santa this may sownd a littel okwerd to you but a wont a computer and a club like captin caivmans Oh by the way this will be my last leter to you all be nine nest year and wont beleve in Santa Claus.

P.S. But I beleve in Santa Claus this year!

Love, Jeff

Dear Santa,

For Christmas I would like a legoe set and a crash up derby. And make lots of noise when you come so I can see you this year.

Your friend, Steve

Dear Santa Claus,

I would like a stereo with a radio and a Record player and things for my train track. I don't know what else because my Birtday is coming up and if I don't get things I want then I'll let you know sos you can bring them for Christmas. If you bring records don't bring the little kids kind.

Love, Kevin

Dear Sana Claus,

I would like a skatebourd and a new bike and perralobarss.

Love, Cheryl

Dear Santa Claus,

I hope you have a nise Christmas. I hope you got a lot of toys becuse there are going to be a lot of chilren hear. I hope you got something reely nice. I hope I can see you on christmas eve. I hope we get a new chrismas tree insted of a new baby lak last year.

Love, Kathleen

Dear Santa Claus:

How are you? I am fine. I don't want much this year but i know my sister does. Here is my list tape recorder, woodstoke puppit, a alesander doll and a lot of jewrie.

Love, Kristin

Dear Santa Claus,

I hope you have a nice Christmas and here are some thing I hope for a football a Aircraft carrier that shote two shotes two planes off it.

Love, Mike

Dear Santa Claws,

I want a hydrocopter and shogun and machie gun and some other stuff that you want to get rid of I hope you are having a nize time at the North Poll.

Love, Mike

Dear Santa,

Are you getting tired of going down the chimny evry year all the time. Why don't one of your helpers do it for you? You can come in our front dor if you want to but dont ring the dorbel youl wake up my dad.

Love Jim

Dear Santa Calus,

I Love Chrsitmas. it is the best holiday. I wish you could come more ofen. How abot Ester or in the sumer anytimes fine with me.

Sin seerly, Robert

Deare Santa Claus,

I want 1000 frate trains and 72 cars and 80 boxes of candy and a hole bunch of toys that wont brake. And hurry.

Your frend, Patrick

Hi Santa,

How have you been this year? Well im fine. Well its Christmas and you are going to bring some toys and a lot of other things. And im going to be glad and so are you. And a lot of other kids are going to be glad to. Well ill be seeing you.

signed Kevin

Dear Santa,

I want a Barbie Doll and a Barbie car and a Barbie howse but I dont want a Ken hes dumb.

Thank you Nancy

Dear Santa Claus,
   How are you? and how are your elvs? I'm just
fine. It is snowing down here and I hope we
have a blizzard so we don't have to go to school
tomorrow.

                                    from Tricia.

Dear Santa:
   I want a skateboard and a radio and a game
called dungon and dragons and if I thing of
some more I will rite again from

                                    Mary

Dear Santa Claus:
   I like you becus you give out prezts. You are
vaire nice to be my dad.

                                    Love Danny

Deer Santa Claws:
   This is dumb becuz I know there isn't no
Santa Claws. If you are relly Santa Claws pruv
it bring me lots of toys!

                                    Tom

Dear Santa Clas,
   Whin you com to our hose don't com down
our chemny becuz it gos to the furnis and you
will burn up! Cum to the front dor and my dad
will let you in. Merry Christmas!

                                    Your frend Francis

Dear Santa,

I want a stawbarry shotcake gane a doll that drings milk a puppy a bird siming gear a ski gear a play house

Sincerely, Jennifer

dear santa

I want a cat a mickey mouse that talks a swimming pool a dog that walks.

Teddy

Dear Santa Claus,

I hope you come this yere Santa. Becas I like you. I like Christmas. I want a new Bike and a camrea to. I want a new rateeto and some shreinkedings to goodby.

from Melanie

Dear Santa,

I would like a Dapper Dan a boy's doll and some books please. I love you very much. I would like a tabblet of papper.

love, Dave

Dear Santa Claus,

Here are the drekshuns to my house. Come to Omaha Nebraska then look for a big white house with a dog house in the back and a three wheeler bike in the front. I want a two-wheeler bike because I'm not a little kid anymore.

See ya, Bill

16

"Communicating" with Your Children

~~~~~~

"Teenagers who haven't spoken to their mother in months will find it imperative to talk to her 'immediately! Right now! It's important!' the moment she steps into the bathtub."

~~~~~~

Much has been written lately about the lack of communication between parents and their children. What I can't understand is the conclusion that such "lack" constitutes a problem.

Frankly, I have never found the *lack* of communication with my kids a problem; when they shut up we get along fine. It's when they talk that we get into trouble.

The problem is: we don't speak the same language. My husband and I speak an ancient language called grammatical English, and the kids speak a strange dialect which is difficult to decode because it is based on only four phrases: "Huh," "I dunno," "It's not my turn," and "I do everything around here!" And those phrases must be forced out of them. Most of the time they wander through the house, ever silent, or they speak only to each other, alternating confidential whispers beginning with "Don't tell Mom and Dad but . . ." with loud, wild threats such as "I'M GONNA TELL MOM AND DAD!"

It wasn't always this way. When my children were tiny, they talked to me all the time. Even before they were born, they would respond to such questions as "Are you still there, sweetheart?" with a kick or a poke. And after they were born, we conversed constantly, in a language any mother could understand.

From the age of two till about ten, they never stopped talking. The toddlers would follow me around the house relating in endless detail what took place on "Captain Kangaroo" or "Sesame Street," or telling me what Santa Claus should bring them for Christmas, even though it was only August.

At age five or six they would come bounding in from school, bent on telling me, immediately and incessantly, every single thing that happened at school or on the way home from school, frequently adding some things that didn't happen— "A tiger chased me down Dodge Street" . . . "I got kidnaped by some bad guys but I excaped"—should my attention begin to flag.

But alas, all children eventually reach the age when they no longer want to communicate with their parents, and thus they develop the dialect that drives Mother crazy.

Just last week I tried to initiate a conversation with my daughter, and it went something like this:

Me: "Ann?"

Daughter: "Huh?"

Me: "Will you help me get dinner, please?"

Daughter: "It's not my turn."

Me: "That's right, you helped me last night. It must be Peg's turn. Where is your sister?"

Daughter: "I dunno."

Me: "I don't know either; you c'mon and help me tonight."

Daughter: "I do everything around here!"

We had a teenage son who didn't talk to us for so long we sent him to a psychiatrist. It was a mistake. The psychiatrist taught him how to talk to us. A subsequent conversation went like this:

Me: "Good morning, Son; how was the party last night?"

Son: "What party?"

Me: "The party at Joe's. Didn't you go to a party at Joe's last night?"

Son: "Why do you ask?"

Me: "Because I want to know! I'm interested! I'm your mother; mothers do take an interest in the activities of their sons. Did you go to that party last night or not?"

Son: "Would it make any difference to you if I had not gone?"

Me: "As a matter of fact, yes!"

Son: "Why?"

Me: "Because I see in this morning's paper that the police raided that party and found three kegs of beer in the backyard. Were you drinking beer at that party?"

Son: "Has it been established that I even went to that party? Don't you trust me, Mother? Why are you so suspicious? Does it have something to do with your past? Did you have a wild youth? Would you like to talk about it?"

Me: "NO!"

I paid somebody sixty dollars an hour to teach this kid to talk to me? I'm the one who needs a psychiatrist.

Many parents have trouble communicating with their children because the children misinterpret what their parents say, and vice versa. As one who has spent years talking to uncomprehending children, I hereby offer a few parental phrases that children universally have trouble interpreting:

"It's time to get up." Despite the fact that this phrase is repeated daily for at least two decades, most children never seem to learn what it means. What it means, kids, is this: "Get thy body out of bed, now, this very minute, not ten minutes from now, not by noon, not tomorrow, but NOW."

"It's your turn to do the dishes [or mow the lawn, or clean the garage, or whatever]." This means that the appointed chore is your responsibility. You may beg, bribe, or threaten a sibling to do it for you, but if the job is not done promptly and to parental satisfaction, it will be *your* head on the block.

"Get in early." The term "early" is easily misconstrued. Therefore, it should be noted that when parents say "early" in discussing a curfew, they usually mean "around midnight," not "around dawn."

"How much money will you need?" means how much money will you need for this particular transaction (to buy a new pair of jeans, to go on the class picnic, etc.). It does not mean, How much money will you need to buy happiness for the weekend? If you intend to hit your parents for more money in the foreseeable future, it is best to estimate your

present need to the nearest dollar, if not the nearest penny. (A thousand brownie points if you bring Mom change.)

"Why don't you date So-and-So? She's such a nice girl" does not mean that So-and-So is a drip. It may not even mean that she is nice. It just means that she is clever enough to act nice around your parents. Don't pass up clever girls.

"Don't call home collect unless it is an emergency." The misunderstandings here arise from the different definitions of the word "emergency." Note that the following are *not* emergencies: (a) you just met a terrific senior and you think you are in love; (b) you forgot your tennis racquet and you need it tomorrow so can you buy a new one and charge it; (c) the cafeteria has lousy meals and you need money for "out" food; (d) you are bored. It shall be considered an emergency if: (a) you are in the hospital; (b) you are in jail; (c) you somehow managed to get hold of two extra tickets to the Nebraska-Oklahoma football game; (d) you are homesick.

"No." The opposite of "yes." Webster interprets "no" as "a denial, refusal, negation or dissent." Even in the loosest interpretation "no" cannot mean "maybe," "perhaps," "we'll see," or "wait long enough and maybe Mom will forget she said 'No.'" (Moms never forget their "No's.")

And here are some fledgling phrases parents often have trouble interpreting:

"The teacher is unfair!" The teacher insists that assignments be handed in on time, quizzes be taken on schedule, and classroom clowns cut it out!

"The referee cheated." They lost.

"If I clean up the whole downstairs before Friday, can I have three dollars to go to the ninth-grade skating party?" This only means that Dad must fork over three dollars; it does not necessarily mean that the downstairs will be cleaned up by Friday; or ever, for that matter.

"Nothing's the matter! Leave me alone!" means that her life is an absolute mess and would you please follow her to her bedroom and listen, silently and lovingly, to the whole sad tale.

"Don't worry about it, Dad; it's no big deal" means you'd better start worrying, Dad, because if there was ever a big deal, this is probably it.

"Can I borrow five dollars?" Literal interpretation: "Gimme money." Persons under the age of twenty-one have no conception of the true meaning of the word "borrow." They do not relate it at all to such terms as "loan" or "debt," especially where Dad is concerned. (Moms are a different matter; we call in the debts, even though we sometimes resort to trickery, saying: "I know I told you I'd pay you five dollars to clean the basement. Remember the five dollars you borrowed last week? Now we're even.")

"I'm sorry I'm late, Dad, but the snow is awful; it's really blowing out there; the streets are impossible; there must have been a hundred accidents on Dodge Street; coming down that steep hill, nobody could stop; even the very best drivers were bumping into each other . . ." You guessed it, Dad; another fender-bender.

"Everybody else's parents gave their permission!" They haven't, but they may if you give in.

For those parents who claim their children won't talk to them under any circumstances, I hereby offer some circumstances guaranteed to break down the communications barriers in your homes:

1. If you have tiny children who won't give you their attention, simply place a long-distance telephone call to somebody important, preferably their grandmother. Your toddlers will immediately climb up on your lap and become all ears.

2. If you have older children who avoid you like the plague, buy yourself some expensive bath salts, run a hot tub, and settle in for a long soak. Teenagers who haven't talked to you since their tenth birthday will bang on the door, demanding your immediate attention.

3. Lure your husband into the bedroom and lock the door. The entire family will immediately converge in the hallway, insisting they must talk to you.

4. A surefire method of setting up regular communication with your kids is to get a job in an office which discourages personal phone calls. Your kids will then call you every hour on the hour.

5. The best method of establishing communication with your offspring is to send them away to college, or let them move into an apartment. They can then be counted on to call home frequently (collect, of course) or to drop by the house (at mealtime, naturally) for long chats, during which they will expound at length on what wonderful parents you were, and what happened, because you certainly are spoiling their younger siblings rotten.

While it has taken me years to learn how to communicate with my children, I had no trouble at all establishing immediate communication with my grandchild.

It's true, he can't yet say anything except "Glubby ga gooby," but I know exactly what that means. It means: "I love my grandma."

Why is it that grandchildren are so much smarter than children?

17

On Costumes

~~~~~~

"School-age children who are told by their teachers to bring a specific item to school [be it money, a note, or a caterpillar costume] will not notify their mother of that fact until 8 A.M. of the given day."

~~~~~~

Years ago, when I first read the Jean Kerr classic *Please Don't Eat the Daisies,* I laughed uproariously at that hilarious chapter in which the Kerrs' son Christopher comes home from school and announces that he got a part in the school play, and that he will need a costume for his role as a back tire. Ah, what an imagination! Jean Kerr could certainly think up some silly situations! As if any play would cast a character as a back tire!

By the time I had five kids of my own going to school, I felt I should write to Mrs. Kerr and apologize for my previous assumption that she had made things up. Obviously, she did not have to look to her imagination for ridiculous episodes; they were all too true-to-life. Even the back tire, undoubtedly. Though I did sometimes speculate, as I sat through year after year of school plays, just what play featured her Christopher as a back tire.

Over the years, I have scrounged up more costumes than I care to count, and I can tell you that there have been many occasions when I would have been grateful for something so simple as a back tire.

Certainly, simulating a back tire would have been easier than constructing a caterpillar.

Our daughter Mary had been in high school only a few weeks when she came home and announced that she had to participate in the freshman field-day program, and she was to play the part of a caterpillar.

"A caterpillar?" I asked. "And what are you going to use for a costume?"

"We're supposed to make it," said Mary.

"What do you mean, 'we're'?" I asked in horror. "I don't have the slightest idea how to make a caterpillar costume. Couldn't you be a chocolate-chip cookie instead?"

"Why would I want to be a chocolate-chip cookie?" she asked.

"Because that's what your brother was last year, and I think we've still got the costume. Or how about a shepherd? Or a clown? Or a table?"

"A table?" she asked.

"Yes," I said. "Don't you remember that modernistic play where the kids played the props as well as the people, and Tim was a table?"

"Not really," she replied. "I do remember Patrick's eagle costume, though. We spent days and days gluing feathers on a sheet and ended up with such a mess Dad suggested we just hang a sign around Pat's neck saying: "I'm an eagle, damn it."

"*There's* a thought!" I said hopefully. "How about a sign saying you're a caterpillar?"

"Don't worry about the costume, Mom," said Mary. "I know how to make it; the teacher gave me a pattern and the instructions. All I'll need from you is the money for the material. But I'll need it now, 'cause I have to have the costume ready by tomorrow."

Of course she would have to have it by tomorrow; I have never had a child yet who gave me more than twenty-four hours' notice on something needed for school.

"Just out of curiosity," I asked, "when did you find out that you would need this costume? Last September?"

"Oh, no," she said sincerely. "They just told me about it today. You see, I was originally scheduled to work backstage, so I didn't need a costume. Carol was supposed to be the caterpillar, but she's in the hospital, so the teacher told me to take her place."

"Fine," I said, "now all you have to do is get Carol's costume."

"Are you kidding?" asked Mary. "Carol is four-foot-ten and I am five-foot-six. Can't you see me squeezed into Carol's costume?"

As Mary was all too sensitive about her height, I declined to comment on that ludicrous vision of a size-nine worm in a size-five body. I conceded that she should have her own costume, and gave her the money for the material.

By the time we sat down to dinner, Mary had already cut the pattern and was hard at work at the sewing machine. I must add that the sewing machine was Mary's, a gift from her grandmother, who could never understand how I could raise ten children without ever sewing a stitch. I have never figured out how to work that sewing machine, and God willing, I never shall.

But even at fourteen, Mary was a wizard at the sewing machine, and she worked diligently all evening on her costume. When I went to bed at midnight she was still seated at the machine, and when I came downstairs at six the next morning she was hand-finishing the "furries" on its "head."

I was chagrined that she had had to stay up all night to finish the costume, and I was astounded at the results.

"Why, Mary, this is beautiful!" I exclaimed. "You really are very talented!"

"I am also very tired," she said with a yawn. "I don't have to be at school till nine o'clock, so I think I'll catch a quick nap. Wake me at eight, will you?"

I assured her I would, and she went off to bed.

At eight o'clock I woke her and she mumbled: "Ten more minutes; just gimme ten more minutes." I woke her again at eight-ten, eight-twenty, eight twenty-five, eight-thirty and eight thirty-five. At eight-forty she bounded out of bed yelling: "Why didn't you wake me? I'll be late for field day!"

I left her to get dressed, and a few moments later I heard a wild shriek.

"What's the matter?" I cried, rushing up to her room.

Mary was standing in the middle of her room, too furious to talk. She was wearing the caterpillar costume, which, from the looks of it, would indicate that the worm had begun to turn into a butterfly. From head to toe the brightly colored caterpillar had "opened up."

"What happened?" I asked.

"It ripped!" wailed Mary. "When I zipped it up the whole thing ripped wide open! It's way too small! The teacher must have given me the same size pattern she gave Carol, and I was too rushed to realize it!"

"What are you going to do?" I asked.

"The only sensible thing to do," sighed Mary as she stepped out of the remains of the caterpillar. "I'm going back to bed. If anybody calls, tell them I am metamorphosing; I'll call them back when I come out of my cocoon."

While it didn't seem to bother Mary that she was missing the freshman field day, it bothered me that I had not been more help to her. True, I don't know how to sew, but I do know how to read, and the least I could have done was catch on to the fact that the pattern was the wrong size.

I determined that from henceforth I would be more co-operative when it came to costuming my kids.

And I was. No, I did not learn how to sew. But I did learn to search. When the kids would come home and tell me they needed a costume for this or that, I would call all my friends, relatives, neighbors, and even the costume shops, to find the needed costume. For the next few years I begged, borrowed, rented or bought costumes for chorus girls, music men, saints, sailors, cupids, clowns, and even inanimate objects, which were the idea of some drama coach who liked being difficult.

On rare occasions I even created the costume myself. Such was the case the year Tim came home and told me he had been picked for a part in the Christmas play.

"You won't believe the character I play in the Christmas program," he said.

"If I won't believe it I guess that means you must be an angel," I teased.

"An angel? In a Christmas play? Boy, Mom, you're livin' in the Dark Ages. We don't have angels in the Christmas program anymore. We don't even have Santa Claus anymore!"

"I forgot," I said with a sigh. "We can't have religion and we can't have legend. Just what kind of a Christmas program are they planning, anyway?"

"It's a *Star Wars* Christmas," said Tim. "I have to play the part of a laser beam."

"At last!" I said with a laugh. "A costume I can create all by myself!"

"You can?" asked Tim incredulously. "Are you sure, Mom?"

"Of course," I said. "Just wait and see."

When time came to produce the costume, I handed Tim a three-dollar flashlight and said: "There you go. You're now a laser beam."

"Say, Mom," said Tim, "this isn't a bad idea. The stage is gonna be dark for my scene; this will be perfect! Thanks a lot!"

Unfortunately, it was not perfect after all. But that was

not *my* fault. I wasn't the one who played with the flashlight backstage all through Acts I and II. By the time the laser beam came onstage, nobody could see him. The batteries were dead.

My kids are growing up now, and while I must still produce costumes for high school and college dramatists, I miss the challenge of the kindergarten and primary plays when my kids would come home to tell me they had been chosen to play the part of a moonbeam, a raindrop, a cloud, a pirate, a puppet, Peter Pan, or maybe even God. (God's costume used to be so easy; all you needed was a white sheet and a fake beard. Now it's a lot more complicated, because God has to look like George Burns.)

I was delighted yesterday when my little neighbor, Teddy, came over to consult with me about the costume for his first-grade play.

"I need a costume," said Teddy, "and Mom said I should ask you if you've got one, 'cause you've got all kinds of weird things at your house."

"I'll have to agree with that, Teddy," I said, laughing. "Just what are you going to be in the play?"

"A back tire," said Teddy.

"A back tire!" I exclaimed. "I don't believe it! I've always wondered about that play! What's the name of it, anyway?"

"It's called *Please Don't Eat the Daisies*," said Teddy. "I get to play the part of Christopher playing the part of a back tire. Do you have an old back-tire costume?"

"I'm sorry, I don't, Teddy," I said. "But I'll be happy to help you look for one."

Jean Kerr, I need you . . . !

18

Lady Luckless

~~~~~~

"The only real winner in Las Vegas is the person who can't figure out how to work the slot machines."

~~~~~~

"I've got great news for you, honey," my husband announced one evening last spring. "We're going to Las Vegas!"

"Why?" I asked.

"What do you mean, 'Why?'" he laughed. "You sound like the kids when we told them we were going to take them to Chicago. Wouldn't you like to see Las Vegas? Don't you realize that Las Vegas is a very famous bit of Americana?"

"Las Vegas is not Americana," I said. "It's Americrazy. Why would I want to go to Las Vegas? I don't like to gamble. I don't like to stay up late. I don't enjoy the blue humor in some of those nightclub acts, or appreciate the nudity in others. What else is there to do in Las Vegas?"

"You can eat," he said. "The Tropicana has one of the grandest dining rooms in the country; gourmet food, wonderful wine, and a romantic atmosphere."

"You're tempting me," I admitted.

"And you don't have to gamble," he continued. "You can just sit by the swimming pool, sipping cool drinks and soaking up some of that nonhumid sunshine."

"I'm weakening," I said.

"My final argument," he said, "and one which I am sure will appeal to your housewifely instincts: it's an all-expense-paid trip. A freebie. It won't cost us a cent."

"Sold," I said. "When do we leave?"

I never learn. You'd think that after all my years on the raffle circuit I would have learned that there is no such thing as a "freebie." The only thing I ever got "free" was a chocolate cake that I won at a church bazaar, and when you consider the number of tickets I have bought at church bazaars, that cake cost me approximately four hundred dollars.

Then there was the "tuition-free" scholarship my son won to college. True, the tuition was free, but his "extra-curricular" expenses totaled almost two thousand dollars.

If there is anything less free than a "tuition-free" education, it is an "all-expense-paid" vacation.

True, the airline tickets were paid for by somebody else. True, the suite at our hotel was compliments of the house. True, our meals were included with the suite. True, everything might have been free . . . had I not been held up by the one-armed bandit.

I know; I said I am not a gambler. But playing the slot machines is not gambling. Gambling is putting your money on the cut of a card, the toss of the dice, the spin of a wheel, knowing all the time that it is just possible (not probable, of course, but possible) that you could win. At baccarat a fellow can win. At blackjack a fellow can win. At roulette a fellow can win. Even at keno, somebody sometimes wins. But not at slot machines. Oh, you may think you are winning, but you're not.

I knew I could not win at the slot machines. Why, then, did I let myself be seduced by that bright-eyed, one-armed monster? Why did I stand there like an idiot, feeding it quarter after quarter, knowing that all I would get out of it would be a black right hand and an empty paper cup?

I really did not intend to touch a slot machine. But determined as I was to avoid those one-armed bandits, I discovered as soon as I got off the airplane that no one, no matter how determined, or how dexterous, can avoid the slot machines. They are in front of you and behind you and to the right and to the left of you. They are everywhere. There are slot machines in the airport lobby, in the airport lounge, in the airport lavatory. I put a dime in a machine to dry my hands, and instead of hot air I got two lemons and an orange. If you have to wait very long at the luggage carousel, you may conclude your visit to Vegas before you get out of the airport.

To my surprise, there were no slot machines in the taxi that took us to our hotel. This is not to say that there is no gambling in Las Vegas taxis. The ride itself is a risk. Las Vegas cabbies must take their training in Manhattan, or maybe even Europe. Our cabbie whizzed down Flamingo Road, weaving through the traffic and waving at other cabbies in their cheerful challenge to get there first. On spotting a traffic jam ahead, he pulled onto the sidewalk, where experienced pedestrians simply moved out of his way while he zoomed along, muttering something about "the crazy drivers in this town who insist on stopping for red lights." But I must admit, the odds are good in the taxi game; almost all Las Vegas tourists make it safely to their hotel.

It's when they reach their hotel that they fall into the pit. Literally.

We pushed open the huge glass doors of our casino-hotel, expecting to see a spacious lobby befitting such a magnificent hostelry, and found instead a pit full of people so engrossed in their gambling they wouldn't have looked up if I had danced through that casino stark naked. What should have been a lobby was a room filled with hundreds of slot machines, gaming tables, roulette wheels, change booths, and back in the corner, behind a pot of ivy, what must have been the registration desk, put there for the convenience of any idiot who really came for a room rather than a rackful of chips.

"I am disillusioned," said a fellow tourist as we waited at the desk. "I had always envisioned this casino filled with sophisticated gamblers, dressed in tuxedos or jeweled gowns. Look at those people in their tank tops and tight slacks. They all look like a bunch of hicks from Nebraska!"

"Hold it!" said I, ever loyal to my hometown. "Those are not Nebraska 'hicks.' Nebraska 'hicks' are too busy raising corn and fattening cattle and striking oil to come out here and feed their fortunes to these silly slot machines!"

But of course, there are exceptions to every rule, and I proved to be the exceptional Nebraska hick. Before I even got upstairs, I fell under the spell of the slot machines. There is something about the "plop-plop-plop" of those coins, coupled with the ding-a-ling of the jackpot bells, that breaks the will of the most determined tourist.

Putting one quarter in a slot machine is like putting one potato chip in your mouth. It has to be followed by another, and another, and yet another, until the chips are all gone, and by then you are addicted.

"C'mon, Teresa," begged my husband, "let's get settled in our suite before you start losing our money!"

"But I'm not losing!" I said triumphantly. "I'm winning! Watch this! I can't believe my luck! Every time I pull that handle I win two quarters!"

"But honey," said my husband patiently, "every single time you are putting *three* quarters in. Two for three can hardly be considered winning."

He finally coaxed me away from the machine, but not until I had lost twenty dollars. (I later learned that a twenty-dollar loss is considered a win in Las Vegas.) We went up to our rooms, and the promised penthouse suite was fantastic.

"Hey, isn't this something!" said my spouse. "Look at that view! And try these sofas! Boy, I could spend the whole week right here in this suite!"

"Well, you can loaf if you want to," I said, "but I'm going sightseeing! I understand this town is swarming with stars. I think I'll amble on down to Caesar's Palace and look around for Sinatra or Sammy Davis, Jr. I'll be back in an hour."

Caesar's Palace is everything it claims to be, and more. It is truly a "wonder of the Western world." The vast expanse of incredible architecture is surrounded by landscaped gardens and lovely fountains as beautiful as any I have ever seen, even in pictures. To give the visitor a better view of the magnificent surroundings, the Palace provides a raised, moving sidewalk to carry you across the "courtyard" and right up to the grand entrance.

As I rode the moving sidewalk across the gardens and past the parking lot filled with fancy cars, including a 1930 Stutz Bearcat, I heard a man behind me muttering to his wife:

"You'll notice they make it plenty easy for you to get into this place, but I'll bet it won't be so easy to get out."

He was right. Not only were there no sidewalks moving exitwise from Caesar's Palace, there were no obvious exits.

I didn't realize this immediately, so enchanted was I with the grandeur of this American palace. The casino interested me not at all; a slot machine is a slot machine is a slot machine, as Stein would say. (And oh, what Stein would say about Las Vegas!) But the ambience of the place fascinated me. The glorious furnishings, the glittering chandeliers, the grand staircases, the marble statuary, the salons, the shops, the dining rooms, the bars, the theaters, on and on it went, through this passage, down that arcade, up this escalator, down that staircase, with more and more to see and more and more to enjoy. What a spectacle! No wonder so many performances are filmed at Caesar's Palace; the background alone should win an Emmy.

I wandered around for a while, enjoying the surroundings and the scenery, and searching for the celebrities I was sure would be there. Is that Sinatra getting off that elevator? No, not with that wife. Sinatra's had a lot of wives, but none of them looked like that. Hey! There's Marie Osmond. No, it couldn't be. She's frowning. Glen Campbell! That fellow looks just like Glen Campbell! But then, everybody in Las Vegas looks a little like Glen Campbell. Now, there's a face I know I know! Where have I seen that man? In the movies? On television? On one of the celebrity billboards advertising the shows? I must be staring; he's smiling at me. He's waving! Oh! He's the taxi driver who brought us in from the airport.

Ah, well. So much for celebrities.

It was when I had decided that I had seen enough of Caesar's Palace that I realized there was still more of Caesar's Palace to see. I took an escalator, hoping to find the lobby, and found only a mezzanine off of a small theater; another escalator took me to a shopping arcade. I went around the arcade and found myself back at the escalator. I tried another passage, which led to another escalator, which led to another mezzanine. There were more shops, more salons, more restaurants, and of course, more casinos, but no lobby. I felt like Tom Sawyer trying to find his way out of that cave.

Finally I realized the awful truth. Caesar's Palace, with all its grand entrances, has no exits.

I searched frantically for a phone. I would call my husband. There were no phones. The only machines that take coins in the place are slot machines. I finally found a "house" phone tucked away in a corner, but it had no coin slot, and no dial. I had to go through Caesar.

A sympathetic operator listened to my plea and dialed

my number for me, and I was eventually connected to my own hotel and my own husband.

"Where in heaven's name are you, Teresa?" he asked. "I've been worried to death about you. You've been gone for hours!"

"I am somewhere in Caesar's Palace," I told him, "and I can't find my way out of here."

"Are you trying to be funny, Teresa?" he asked. "Just go to the door and walk out."

"You don't understand," I said. "There aren't any doors. There are just rooms and passageways and slot machines and shops and stairways, but no doors. At least, I can't find any."

"Don't be ridiculous," he said. "Just go to the front lobby and you'll find the front door."

"That's easy for you to say," I said. "You aren't in Caesar's Palace. If there is a lobby in this place, I certainly haven't seen it, and I have been all over the place. I don't think they have a lobby."

"Of course they have a lobby," he said. "Just look around you. When you see daylight, head for it; that's the lobby."

"Daylight!" I wailed. "What's daylight? I haven't seen daylight in the past three hours! There are no windows in this place! There are no windows in the whole of Las Vegas! I tell you, there is no way out!"

Eventually, of course, I found my way out of Caesar's Palace, and I wouldn't go back in there, not even to see Sinatra. If Frankie wants to sing for me, he's going to have to do it on my turf.

Despite the fact that I lost my money, and my self, in Las Vegas, I loved the week we spent there. I loved the lights and the laughter and the glitter and the gaiety, though I did wonder, one midnight as we walked along the Strip, what would happen if someone were to pull the plug on Las Vegas. I envisioned one gigantic fuse, at Hoover Dam perhaps, blowing . . . and leaving Las Vegas blacked out. Can you imagine the lights of Las Vegas darkened, the machines dead, the croupiers unable to see the cards, the tourists unable to see the chorus girls . . . gad, what a disaster movie that would make!

The highlight of our trip, as my husband promised, was dinner at the Tropicana. Perhaps that is Las Vegas as the tourist imagines it to be. The casino seemed more like Monte Carlo, or at least movies of Monte Carlo, and the tuxedos and long, lovely gowns were in abundance. The grand dining room was candlelit, with white linen cloths, sparkling crystal, heavy silver, and a menu filled with gourmet delights. Even the maître d' was perfect, with a European accent, and an Old World manner to match. That's what I will always remember of Las Vegas. The beautiful, bounteous dining rooms beat the casinos, hands down!

"Wasn't it a terrific week?" I told my husband when we got home. "And to think it was free!"

"Well, actually, it wasn't entirely free," he said.

"What do you mean?" I asked. "Our air fare was paid for, our hotel was paid for, our meals were included in the package, even our tips were covered. What do we have to pay?"

"The taxes," he said. "We won that trip, you know; we have to pay taxes on it, just as if it were income."

"That's absolutely ridiculous," I said. "But I guess we will have to pay them. Say . . . you don't suppose the Internal Revenue Service would want to go for double or nothing?"

19

On Shopping
for Clothes

*"The surest way to find a winter coat on sale is
to have bought it yesterday for full price."*

"I think people should boycott the clothing stores," I told my
husband as I sank wearily into the sofa and kicked off my
shoes.

"It looks like you have already boycotted them," he said.
"What other wife would go shopping with a blank checkbook
and come home empty-handed? And you've only been gone
a couple of hours! I thought you'd stay out all afternoon and
come home loaded with boxes of new clothes. Don't tell me
you didn't buy anything."

"I didn't buy anything," I admitted, "and you wouldn't
have stayed out as long as I did if you had been in my shoes
. . . literally, that is. Just look at my swollen feet! Do you
have any idea how painful it is to walk around for two hours
in four-inch heels?"

"Why do you go shopping in heels?" he asked. "You
knew you'd be walking for hours."

"I have to wear heels to shop for dressy clothes," I explained. "One can hardly try on dressy clothes while wearing tennis shoes. Though it didn't really make any difference, because, as it turned out, I didn't try on any clothes at all."

"Why not?" he asked. "Couldn't you find anything you liked?"

"I couldn't even find anything I didn't like," I said with a sigh. "I was looking for a winter coat and a good wool suit, and this being the middle of January, they naturally didn't have any winter coats or wool suits in stock. All they stock in January are summer dresses and swimsuits. And that's why I think people should boycott the shops until they shape up and sell winter clothes in winter and summer clothes in summer. Who can get enthusiastic about swimwear when it's snowing outside? And who wants to try on fur coats in the middle of August?"

"Almost any woman but you," he said. "You amaze me; you are the only woman I know who doesn't care anything about clothes."

My husband is right. I simply do not have any interest in fashions, styles, or who is wearing what this season. While most wives would be thrilled to have their husbands send them out shopping, I would be much happier if somebody would buy my clothes for me and just bring them home and hang them in my closet. I would wear them cheerfully and without complaint, oblivious to how they look or even if they fit. It would be enough that I did not have to traipse from shop to shop, sorting through rack after rack, trying on one outfit after another, while all the time being forced to look in that dreadful three-way mirror which confirms my suspicions that the back of me is getting bigger than the front.

I think my apathy concerning clothes may be due to the fact that I spent half my life in school uniforms and the other half in maternity clothes.

There is nothing that makes a girl feel less glamorous

than a school uniform. I think the concept behind a school uniform was to make all the girls look alike, and thus no girl would ever feel that she was less pretty than her peers. And it worked. We all looked equally ugly. Made of stiff, navy-blue serge, our uniforms wore like iron, and felt like it too. The heavy, scratchy skirt and bolero were equaled in discomfort only by the highly starched, unbecoming (but definitely modest!) blouse. Neither the skirt nor bolero nor blouse fit properly, probably because their very durability caused our mothers to buy them "a little large so you can grow into them." When I was six years old I dragged around in a skirt that had a hem eight inches deep; by the time I entered sixth grade, the hem had decreased to half an inch, but I was still wearing that same skirt, and if it were around today I am sure that my daughter could wear it. ("Could," not "would." Today's strong-willed daughters wouldn't be caught dead in such an outfit.)

The only reason I did not wear that same skirt throughout high school was that the high school uniform was a different style (or so they claimed). It had supposedly been designed with the fashion-conscious teenager in mind, but that was really a waste of time and effort because, after spending eight years in the awful blue-serge grade-school uniform, we girls had long since lost consciousness as far as fashion was concerned.

The teenage skirt and bolero were also made of that dreadful navy-blue serge (gad, how we hated that scratchy material; the nuns said it was chosen for its "warmth and wearability," but the students claimed that Reverend Mother's brother sold the stuff) and looked absolutely awful on everybody, with the possible exception of Virginia Hartigan, who would have looked good in a potato sack.

On graduation, I joyfully burned my uniform, and as a reward for my long-suffering years in uniform, my parents outfitted me with a beautiful, expensive and stylish college wardrobe. There was only one problem. That was the year of the New Look, when almost-to-the-ankle skirts were "the thing to wear," and since they had been so expensive, I wore them for the next four years, despite the fact that hemlines rose drastically by my junior year. But that didn't bother me a bit; so what if my clothes weren't stylish? At least they weren't blue serge!

My mother tried again to turn me into a fashion plate when I got married. In buying my trousseau, she insisted that I "get the very best, but this time choose traditional fashions that will always be in style." So I bought handsome tailored suits, beautiful blazers and skirts, daytime and cocktail dresses and sports clothes galore, but I never got to wear most of them, because after the first sixth months of marriage I was always in maternity clothes.

Now, I will be the first to acknowledge that maternity fashions have come a long way in style and design since the sack dress and the smock, but they are still maternity clothes, and nobody can feel glamorous in a garment she has worn one hundred and ninety-two times, especially when she can see her waistline without even looking down. Now, it's true that I only wore maternity clothes for twelve years, but I wore them so continuously I certainly felt that I had worn them for always.

As my mother predicted, even after twelve years my trousseau clothes were still in style, but what she had not predicted was that they would not fit. (I defy anybody to go through ten pregnancies and end up a size six!) So I was forced to spend the next few years painfully replenishing my wardrobe, and even though my fashion demands were few (it must have a belt and it can't be blue serge), I dreaded shopping because I could never seem to find anything truly becoming.

While I find shopping for clothes frustrating, sorting and

choosing and making decisions is not nearly as difficult as paying for the darn things. It's not so much the high prices that get to me as it is the red tape involved in completing a purchase.

"Will this be cash or charge?" the clerk will ask when I finally decide that the gray wool doesn't look quite as bad as the red gabardine, and I never know how to respond, because I intend to pay by check, which technically is not cash (and, in my case sometimes, isn't even backed by cash). I never pay by cash, because many of the younger clerks get confused when they have to handle real money, and I refuse to use my charge accounts because, as anybody who has ever found herself making monthly payments on her finance charges knows, therein lies bankruptcy. So, as the lesser of three evils, I write a check, and therein lies insanity. A shopper can go berserk just waiting for her check to be approved.

If they ever get to the check. You can grow old and die just waiting for the clerk to write up the ticket. This is not the clerk's fault; it is the fault of some unknown idiot who, in trying to create a monster, came up with something almost as ghoulish: computerized merchandising.

Before the clerk can even write up the ticket, she must first tear about seventeen little tags off the garment (including, you hope, the tag that sets off an alarm if it is carried out of the store). Then she must consult a series of charts and ledgers in order to cross-check the torn-off tags with codes which will identify the type of garment, manufacturer, material, style, and whether or not it will fall apart before it shrinks or vice versa. Another chart must be consulted to determine the date, time, place and department of purchase, as well as the identification number of the salesclerk. (Yes, it's her own number, but in all this mess, you certainly don't expect her to remember it, do you?) Still another ledger must be checked to see if the price marked on the garment is current, or if perhaps it is on sale. (You can bet it isn't; you just happened to choose the one garment that "just came in today; it shouldn't have been on that sale rack.")

When the salesclerk has completed all the checking and rechecking, she must then punch all the data into a computerized cash register which is programmed to catch any errors, answer any questions, and, I have always suspected, shout: "Bloomingdale, T. No credit, no checks. Prosecute," on those days that my children have preceded me on a shopping spree.

If and when the clerk gets all the data correctly into, and out of, the computer, she will then tell me the price of the garment, and only after I have written half the check will she add: ". . . plus two twenty-eight in tax," thus requiring me to tear up that check and write another.

As she takes my check, she then makes the statement I most dread hearing:

"I'll have to get this approved."

She then disappears into the back of the store, where, I have always suspected, she eats her lunch, reads one or two chapters of *Die with Desire,* makes an after-five date with the assistant manager and finally remembers to get his okay on my check.

You think that's it? I mean, do you think that at this point I can take my crummy purchase and go home? Absolutely not! For while the check has been approved, I have yet to prove that I am me and the check is mine!

In other words, I must produce three acceptable pieces of identification.

I have learned, through many embarrassing, humiliating, and frustrating transactions, that the following are not "acceptable" pieces of identification: the little white card that came with your billfold and on which you carefully typed all the suggested data identifying you; your library card; your PTA membership card; an unpaid traffic ticket; pictures of your children (even if they look like you); the little plastic card with your picture on it that you paid ten dollars for because the vendor convinced you that you would need it when you try to cash a check. The only acceptable pieces of identification are: a driver's license and two major bank credit cards.

But you need three pieces of identification, and who carries *two* major bank credit cards? I'll tell you who: credit risks and criminals. I once stood in line behind a fellow who wrote a check for $400 worth of purchases, and I thought surely the clerk would be suspicious when this customer cheerfully pulled out his billfold and produced all kinds of proper identification. I mean, what *honest* man is willing to go through all that rigmarole? The customer completed his purchase and made his getaway before the clerk thought to check that under-the-counter ledger (in which I am sure my name will be entered someday if it isn't already) and discovered that all of those credit cards, as well as the driver's license, had been reported stolen.

Only the bad guys can get away with that, however. On another occasion I was behind a well-dressed gentleman, a prominent lawyer in the community, who wanted to write a check for a $20 shirt he had just purchased. When the clerk asked for identification, the man grumbled a bit, but pulled out his wallet and produced a Visa card, a birth certificate, a lodge card with his picture on it, his membership cards in the American Bar Association, the state Bar Association and the Association of Trial Lawyers of America, plus four sales receipts from the very next department showing that he had just charged over $300 worth of purchases on his store account. He also had a bankbook with his name, address, Social Security number and phone number, showing a savings account balance exceeding $10,000.

Yet the clerk refused to cash his check because this well-dressed, well-known, well-heeled gentleman didn't have a driver's license.

I thought he might get angry with her, but he didn't; blind persons seldom lose their temper.

20

On Horoscopes

~~~~~~

"No matter what sign you were born under, everybody else's horoscope will be more fun than yours."

~~~~~~

I hate to admit this, but I am hooked on horoscopes. I know that horoscopes are as silly as soap operas, but like the people who mock such shows as "Dallas" and "Ryan's Hope" and "As the World Turns," and then watch them religiously, I will scoff at moon signs and planetary rulers and rising signs, and then give my undivided attention to anything or anybody who even pretends to predict my future.

Which is ridiculous, because if there is anything I really don't want to know, it is my future. I find it hard enough to cope with my present, thank you, and if I had foreseen my past when it was still my future, I certainly would have done everything in my power to prevent it from becoming my present.

As a matter of fact, I have lived long enough that I do not need the moon or the stars to tell me what is going to happen this afternoon or tomorrow or next week. I already *know* what is going to happen.

For example, at approximately one-thirty this afternoon the school nurse is going to call me to tell me that one or the other of my children, all of whom went off to school this morning hale and hearty, is deathly ill and must be picked up immediately. I know this will happen because at one o'clock this afternoon I will be entertaining twenty guests at a luncheon I have been planning for months.

As for tomorrow, well, let me tell you what the planets predict for my tomorrow: "A humiliating situation may result from a disagreement in regard to finances." Of course, there will be a disagreement about finances tomorrow. Tomorrow is the first of the month, and half the check writers in America will be joining me in calling the bank to argue that our statements are in error. And we all know that it won't be the bank who ends up humiliated.

And next week? My horoscope predicts that I "may have to take on more responsibilities because of slow-moving associates." To a mother of six live-in children, that isn't a prediction; it's a fact of life.

One thing that bugs me about horoscopes is the fact that everybody else's is more fun than mine. I always seem to get the "dire circumstances" and "family crises" and "unforeseen expenditures," while my family and friends can count on "profitable enterprises" and "romantic relationships" and "fulfillment of innermost desires." Now tell me, is that fair? Frankly, I think we Leos should protest. As "good-natured, optimistic, positive" people we are not prepared for those problems. Give them to the Virgos. Those "pessimistic, anxious, cautious" fellows expect the worst anyway; why disappoint them with pleasant surprises?

Just last week my Virgo husband was promised a day of "mystery, intrigue and romance." Was he excited about it? Of course not. (Though I must say, he wasn't his usual pessimistic self after hearing that prediction.) He wasn't even interested, while I, on the other hand, would have been ecstatic with such a forecast. And what did the planets hang on me that day? "View emotional issues in the proper perspective." I knew what *that* meant; I wasn't supposed to make waves about You-Know-Who's mysterious, intriguing romance. But my determination to cooperate with my moon sign was for naught; when my husband came home he told me that if there had been any intrigue or romance in his day, it had remained a mystery to him. Of course it had. Virgos are so skeptical they wouldn't recognize a proposition if they got one.

Despite my tendency to pooh-pooh planetary predictions, I must admit that it is amazing how often a daily horoscope comes true. Whether this is due to coincidence or broad interpretation, the fact remains, the predictions are often fulfilled.

For example, one Monday morning my horoscope hinted that I would "come into some money from an unexpected source," and sure enough I did. Tim paid me back the buck I had loaned him the day before, and if ever there was an "unexpected source" of money, it is a fourteen-year-old boy who owes his mother a dollar.

The very next day my horoscope read: "A financial loss will come as no surprise." And I will certainly admit that it was no surprise when I opened my purse and found that somebody had filched the dollar I had placed there yesterday.

Wednesday's horoscope predicted that my "social life would accelerate," a suggestion that intrigued me until I remembered that Wednesday was the day I had to chaperone the fifth grade on a field trip to the zoo. My social life did indeed accelerate . . . from the snack bar to the monkey pit and back again.

Thursday's horoscope warned me that "a frantic relative will ask for money." So what else is new? In this household of always-broke, ever-begging teenagers I would be relieved if that prediction could be limited to Thursdays.

On Friday I read my horoscope and was delighted to see

that, at last, I got a good one. "Chance of travel, change of scenery possible. An old romance could bring you happiness." Well, I must say: it's about time!

"Hey, look at this!" I told Old Romance when he came down to breakfast. "My rising sign finally rose. Let's go someplace this weekend, just you and I. The kids can take care of themselves . . ."

Before I could continue, my husband peered over my shoulder at the newspaper and read *his* horoscope, which could only make me wonder how the stars know who is married to whom.

He read aloud: "Mate may make unreasonable demands. Be firm. Offer irrefutable arguments in your favor."

"I know you don't like these spur-of-the-moment vacations," I said, "but I can't believe that you can come up with one good argument as to why we can't take off for the weekend!"

Whereupon he silently pointed to yet another horoscope, that of our teenage son. It read: "Surprise may be on the horizon; accent on pleasure. Eat, drink and make merry!"

Then, as if that wasn't argument enough, he pointed to my horoscope for the following Monday. It read: "Home repairs may be necessary."

You guessed it. We stayed home.

A recent bit of advice from my horrible horoscope suggested: "Perhaps you should consider a name change." A name change? Who needs a new name? What I need is a new birthday!

While some people are intrigued with their future, others make a hobby of trying to interpret their dreams.

Have you ever wondered why we all have the same nightmares? For example, there is the common dream where we find ourselves at the Elks Club Ball, or in the middle of Sunday church services, dressed only in our underwear or

nightgown or maybe even less. People who have this dream
(and who doesn't?) often blame their mothers, who spent
their childhood warning: "Wear clean underwear so you
won't be embarrassed when you get hit by a truck and have to
disrobe in the emergency ward." But the truth is, of course,
that both the guy in his shorts and the gal in her nightie are
so clothed in their dreams because that is what they are wearing when they have those dreams. It's as simple as that.

Another common nightmare is the one in which we are
running with leaden feet, trying to elude a vicious assailant
who is following close on our heels. When I was young I had
that dream all the time, but it terminated one night not long
ago when I dreamed that I was running, running, running
with leaden feet and finally decided to hell with it; I'm too old
for this sort of thing. So I stopped, turned around and said: "I
give up! Take me! I'm yours!" And do you know that jerk
passed me by without so much as a pardon me? (Thereby
fulfilling my brother's long-ago prediction: "Don't worry, Sis;
he'd leave you at the first lamppost.")

My worst nightmare is one in which my mother comes to
visit and asks to see the new baby, and I shout: "My God, the
baby! I forgot we had a new baby! I haven't fed her since
Wednesday!" It's truly a terrible dream, and I cannot explain
it, for I was most conscientious about feeding my babies,
though said "babies" would have you believe I have since
starved them to death.

My most recurring nightmare, however, is one which
certainly needs no explanation. I am standing at the kitchen
sink, washing dish after dish after dish, while dirty plates and
cups and cereal bowls reproduce themselves on the counters
around me. This nightmare got so exhausting one night, I
pleaded with my husband: "I can't stand this anymore! Wake
me up! Wake me up!"

Whereupon my husband came out into the kitchen and
asked:

"What's the matter with you? You *are* awake!"

21

Whence Go Athletes

~~~~~~

"An eight-year-old boy who is too tired to empty wastebaskets at 4 P.M. will somehow find the energy to play nine innings of baseball at 4:30."

~~~~~~

I have never been able to understand this country's rather manic idea that every little boy should be an athlete. It's comparable to the equally ridiculous theory that every little boy should have a dog. Who says? I'll tell you who says: Dad says. You can be sure it wasn't Mom. Even mothers who are enthusiastic football fans would prefer that it not be their sons who are down on the field getting mangled and mauled and thrown for a loss. Better their son should play in the band, participating in the festivities but not in the injuries.

In fact, if mothers had their way, their sons would start, at a very early age, to appreciate the finer things of life, like music and art and how to help around the house, with childhood sports limited to sandlot baseball, free tennis in the park, and swimming in a pool close enough to walk to.

But fathers seem to be obsessed with football, baseball and basketball, and the moment they hear that magic phrase

"Congratulations, sir; your wife just had a bouncing baby boy!" they run right out and buy something for the kid to bounce, or bat, or kick.

I first realized that my husband had athletic aspirations for his sons when he could not wait for our oldest son to earn his first letter sweater; he bought him one. I admit it was a beautiful sweater, heavy-knit, in that bright University of Nebraska red, with one side left blank for the yet unearned letter, and the other side proudly emblazoned: "Class of '77." The sweater was even stylishly large, being a size one, while our "athlete" was still wearing infant shirts size zero to three months.

While our son did wear that sweater all through his first winter, he had outgrown it before the fall of '57, but that was all right because by that time he refused to wear anything other than his "batheball thute," complete with visored cap and waterproof knickers.

In the next three years we had three more sons, convincing my husband that perhaps a team was in the making. Consequently the stuffed animals and alphabet blocks I had purchased were cast aside in favor of sponge footballs, plastic baseballs, multicolored basketballs, and, for the baby, a teething ring in the shape of a tennis racquet. Our living room looked like a gymnasium. (Smelled like one too.)

My husband was absolutely dedicated to his determination to make athletes out of our sons. As soon as each baby was old enough to toddle out into the backyard, my husband would take him outside and teach him how to hit a baseball. Unfortunately, he only taught him *how* to hit, not *where* to hit, and for the next few years we had baseballs flying through our kitchen windows, our car windows, and, as the kids grew older and stronger, the neighbors' windows. The local glazier loved us; we made him rich.

While the boys loved baseball and basketball (will I ever stop hearing "thump-thump-thump-thump"? Will the neighbors ever stop complaining about our "thump-thump-thump-thump"?), they were more enthused about football. There was little danger of my toddlers kicking the ball through my windows, because they seldom bothered to kick the football, or for that matter, even touch the football. They were not interested in kicking field goals or completing forward passes or even making touchdowns; all they wanted to do was kick, punt, block and tackle each other. Football is a little boy's dream come true. They can wrestle and roll and knock each other down and about, all in the name of athletics. What fun! What noise! What blood!

Needless to say, I hated it. I hated it not so much because I feared they would get hurt (if they didn't get hurt playing football they would get hurt falling off their trikes or out of trees; it was six of one and half a dozen of the other) as because I feared they would become addicted to athletics, and once they started to school they would get lost in that labyrinthian horror: organized sports.

Every mother who has ever had a child involved in school athletics knows what "organized sports" entails: scheduled practices and unscheduled meals and confusing car pools and angry parents and tearful right-fielders who wonder why everybody keeps yelling at them and for cryin' out loud, how is a guy expected to catch a fly ball with the sun in his eyes?

What ever happened to sandlot ball, where the little kids in the neighborhood just got together and played ball down on the corner lot, with no rules, no uniforms, and most important, no adults? I don't know at what point in time it was decided that games for kids six, seven and eight years old should be "organized," but I wish a pox on whoever decided the games must be played on a regulation field, with the players wearing expensive uniforms, obeying strict rules, following an inflexible lineup and somebody necessarily keeping score. Nothing ruins a little boy's baseball game so much as keeping score.

Though I must admit it is rather intriguing to watch the scoring at a little boys' baseball game. With many of the boys still too uncoordinated to connect bat to ball, it is not so much a question of keeping score as it is making a score. One Cub Scout league I know finally passed a rule that the game must end after the sixth inning (even if the score is tied 0–0), or if one team gets thirty points ahead of the other. I watched one game between the first and second grade that was called because of darkness . . . in the second inning.

It's not that the little boys are such terrible players; some of them are really rather good (thus necessitating the 30-plus rule); it's just that they are so nervous and uptight, with the parents standing on the sidelines yelling and screaming and threatening to put them up for adoption if they strike out.

What on earth happens to parents at little league games? I have watched the most genteel, sweet-tempered mother turn into a witch when an umpire dared to call her little darling "Out!" And I have seen a father, whom I know to be the soul of dignity and diplomacy at the office and sometimes even at home, rant and rave because his seven-year-old son failed to catch an easy fly ball. I have known neighbors who have been good friends for years to stop speaking to each other simply because their sons played on rival teams. I have even known a married couple who stopped speaking to each other because they couldn't agree on whether or not their son should have attempted to steal third base. And that was why I stopped going to those baseball games . . . not because I couldn't bear to see all those people act like idiots, but because I couldn't keep *my* mouth shut.

To be honest, I stopped going to the games because I couldn't get out of my car long enough to watch a game. At one point, six of our children were involved in little league baseball (by this time the girls were as active in athletics as the boys), and I spent the entire summer in my car, driving various players to various game sites, and then retracing my route to pick them all up again. As I recall, that was the summer of the gasoline shortage. (Now you know what caused it.)

Baseball was not my only *bête noire*. Soccer came in a close second.

When my firstborn child started in school, soccer was a European sport little known in the United States. By the time my tenth child started in school, soccer had not only been introduced into our elementary schools, it had become as popular as spitballs. Every kid wanted to be on a soccer team, and every team wanted to play every day. Games were scheduled almost every evening during the soccer season (which lasted, as any soccer mother can tell you, about fourteen months out of the year), and on weekends the games ran from eight o'clock in the morning till dusk.

Since every child in our neighborhood had signed up to play soccer somewhere, we mothers finally organized car pools, which became so busy and so efficient we could have put any major metropolitan transit system to shame.

I shared one car pool with my neighbor Jean, whose daughters Kyle and Jenny played on the same teams with my daughters Peggy and Annie. I shared another car pool with my friend Sue, whose sons Mike and Bob played on teams with my sons Tim and Patrick. And sometimes, if their games coincided with those of my children, I would drive David and Jennifer, children of next-door-neighbor Mary Jo, along with my friend Shari's sons, Dirk and Eric, who went to a different school but played in the same league. We had a huge station wagon, and the kids didn't seem to mind being crowded, so it worked out very well . . . until the last Saturday of the season.

The season had been hectic, with rainy weather causing games to be postponed and rescheduled, only to be postponed again. By the final weekend the kids still had four games to play in order to qualify for the tournament.

My Peg had to play at eight o'clock in the morning, at a field out in west Omaha, while Annie had a game scheduled at the same time at a field in east Omaha. Since Jean's daughter Kyle was on the same team with Peg, Jean said she would drive to west Omaha, while I agreed to take her daughter Jenny to east Omaha, along with my daughter Ann, and Sue said she would pick them up and bring them home when she took her Bob and my Patrick to their game, which was at the same field but two hours later.

That was great, since I knew I wouldn't be able to pick them up because I would be taking Sue's Mike and my Tim to their game in south Omaha, which was close to the field where Dirk was playing, and David was playing there too, so I would take them also. Dirk's brother Eric was playing in a game close to Bob and Pat's, so Sue said she would take Eric when she took Bob and Pat. Dirk's mother, Shari, offered to pick them all up, but Mary Jo said no, she would because she had to pick up Jennifer anyway, and I said that was silly; Jennifer was playing just across the street from Patrick and I could pick her up, along with Dirk and David, when I picked up Bob, Pat and Eric. Jean had already said she would pick up and bring home Peg and Kyle, so Mary Jo and Shari said they would handle all the driving the next day.

I know it sounds very complicated, but it was really very simple and it all worked out beautifully. Everybody got to their games on time, and everybody got picked up on time. There was only one slight hitch. By the time I got home, after depositing various children in various homes, I ended up with two Jennifers and a Bob, but no Peg, Ann, Tim or Patrick.

"Don't worry about it," said my husband with a laugh, when he found me banging my head on the steering wheel of my car.

"What do you mean, don't worry about it?" I wailed. "I've deposited kids all over the neighborhood who probably don't even live there, and where on earth are our kids? How am I ever going to get this all straightened out?"

"Simple!" he said. "Just throw them all back in the car pool tomorrow, and let Shari and Mary Jo sweat it out. I guarantee, we'll get our own kids back!"

Of course we did, and to my great relief they all outgrew their addiction to athletics. None of my children has been tackled on the football field in high school or college, and they all seem to be headed for genteel careers in insurance, law, engineering and teaching. One son has even been dabbling in creative writing, and he called home from college recently to tell us he had sold an article to a magazine for the magnificent sum of $500.

"Aren't you proud of him?" I asked my husband when I gave him the news. "Just think, five hundred dollars! I bet his classmates are green with envy!"

"All but Vince," he said.

"Vince Who?" I asked.

"You know, that nice kid who dropped out of college to play pro football. Last I heard, he signed with the NFL for three hundred thousand a year."

Somehow I wish he hadn't told me that. But also somehow, I knew he just had to!

22

The Demise of the CIA

"He who claims his child never lies, lies."

The CIA has met its match . . . or is about to, and I must admit I feel sorry for them. I have matched wits with their future adversaries, and I wouldn't wish that battle on anybody, not even the CIA.

I am referring to the recent reports that the CIA will be allowed to investigate domestic as well as foreign affairs, and in so doing, I assume they will, at some point, choose to investigate the personal quirks, shady transactions, and clandestine affairs of America's young adults, or worse, America's adolescents. God help them. (The CIA, that is; the adolescents will enjoy the whole bit.)

I don't know whether or not I agree with the theory that our security is more important than our privacy, and that the CIA should thus be allowed to spy on us (I can only think of Pogo: "We have met the enemy and they is us"); but the question is moot, for once the CIA investigations have reached the younger generation, that notable and notorious "company" will be all through.

I base this assumption on the fact that I have spent years spying on the younger generation, and have acquired nothing but a stomach ulcer, migraine headaches, and an occasional twitch over my left eye. Kids are masters at avoiding interrogation, suppressing a search, and concealing relationships. It's not that they lie; it's just that they circumvent the truth by playing ignorant or innocent, neither of which they ever are.

Frankly, I would love to listen to a CIA agent trying to interrogate any one of my daughters, assuming, of course, that he could catch one of my daughters long enough to interrogate her. The interrogation would undoubtedly go something like this:

"You are M. T. Bloomingdale; is that correct?"

"Hmmm? Oh. Hi. What was it you asked?"

"Your name. What is your name?"

"My name? Antigone!"

"Who?"

"Antigone! I am Antigone, daughter of Oedipus, Sophocles' greatest heroine!"

"I must be in the wrong house; I'm looking for the Bloomingdales."

"Unfortunately, this *is* the Bloomingdales. Do you have any idea how difficult it is to assume the personality of a dramatic character in this insane household? In order to play Antigone, I must *be* Antigone! At least until the play is over; the play's the thing!"

"Let's try this again. Are you or are you not M. T. Bloomingdale?"

"M.T.? Let me think a minute . . . Mother? What's my middle name again? Oh. Yeah. I guess I am M. T. Bloomingdale. But I'm not the Bloomingdale you want. Try M.G. Or M.M."

"How do you know you're not the one I want?"

"Because whatever it is, I didn't do it, and if it's something that needs doing, it's not my turn. Now, if you'll excuse me, I'm late . . ."

"And where are you going?"

"Out."

"Out where?"

"Out there! Why do I have to give a detailed report every time I go anyplace? How old does a girl have to be before she can live her own life? I'm going out with a guy; we're just going out for a drink, and then maybe on to a show. Now if you will please excuse me . . ."

"What guy? What's his name?"

"If you must know, his name is Bill."

"Bill Who? What's his last name?"

"I don't know his last name. What difference does it make? 'What's in a name?' Next thing you'll be asking is 'What does his father do?' Bill's just a guy I met at work; I don't run a credentials check on every guy I go out with!"

"Where are you and this Bill going?"

"I don't see that it's any of your business; but if you must know, we're going to my place."

"You mean . . . here?"

"Are you crazy? I wouldn't bring anybody back here! I've got too many brothers and sisters around here; and worse, I've got parents! Do you know how embarrassing it is to be twenty-one years old and living with your parents?"

"But you said you were going to *your* place. Am I to assume that you have an apartment hideaway? For assignations or rendezvous?"

"Hardly. I said I was going to My Place; My Place is a neighborhood bar. It's a great place for happy-hour drinks . . . half price. Or at least they will be, if I get there before happy hour is over."

"I just have one more question. Have you and this fellow Bill at any time ever discussed the destructive capabilities of the Soviet-built laser-bearing interplanetary satellite missile?"

"Oh, absolutely; all the time. That's our favorite topic of conversation."

"I am not joking. Do you realize what it would mean if these weapons were ever put to use?"

"Yeah. It'd mean good-bye earth, hello heaven . . . and it would also mean we'd better eat, drink and be merry while we can, right? Want to come along to My Place?"

If the interrogations don't drive the CIA out of business, the searches will. I defy any CIA agent to find anything at all in a typical teenager's bedroom, except of course those things which are usually found in a teenager's bedroom, a list of which would be too long to mention here.

Can't you just imagine a couple of CIA agents trying to find something in the bedroom of a seventeen-year-old boy? The scenario might well go like this:

The handgun law has been passed, probably with weapons of all kinds addended, and two secret agents have just broken into the bedroom of a high school senior, male, age seventeen, who, it goes without saying, is not present . . . it not being between the hours of 1 A.M. and noon.

"We can't get in; the door is locked."

"It can't be locked; the new law forbids the locking of bedroom doors. Maybe it's blocked; let me try. Yeah, you gotta shove; there's a couple of things in the way" (a foot locker, guitar case, typewriter stand, fourteen library books, and six and a half pairs of gym shoes).

"I got it; here we go. AAAGGHH! Grab your gas mask! The room is filled with poison gas!"

"That's not poison gas; that's dirty socks. I've got a kid of my own; can't stand to go in his room. Okay, what are we looking for?"

"Anything illegal; weapons, drugs, acid-rock records. Just start looking and let me know if you find anything at all that looks suspicious. You search the desk and I'll take the closet."

"That's not fair; you know there won't be anything in the closet. What kid ever hangs up his clothes?"

"Okay; I'll take the drawers, and you search under the bed."

"Are you crazy? I'm not going under there. I didn't volunteer for Perilous Projects; I'm not trained for hazardous duty. Anyway, we've only got eight hours; it'd take two days to sift through that stuff. You take the bureau drawers; I'll take the desk. Hey, look here; this looks like a secret document. It's in some kind of code."

"That's just a term paper, dummy; can't you see the grade in the margin? The kid got an A."

"Naw, this has got to be code. Look how all the words are misspelled, and there are commas and periods in ridiculous places. Read it; it doesn't even make sense. If it's a school term paper, how could the kid have gotten an A on it?"

"Simple. He's a football player. Now c'mon; we gotta search. Hey, look what I found in this bureau drawer! The Director isn't gonna believe this!"

"What is it? All I see are socks and underwear."

"I know. That's what I mean. Suspicious, huh? What teenage kid keeps his socks and underwear in his bureau drawer? I tell you, there's something funny going on here! Let's see what he's got buried under these clothes . . . awwggh! I've been wounded! There is a weapon in here!"

"You call that a weapon? It looks like a mousetrap to me. Hey, it's got a note attached to it. What does it say?"

"Sis: don't say I didn't warn you! Keep out of my stuff!"

"Aha! And what's the 'stuff' he's hiding from his sister? Let's dig a little deeper . . . here! . . . what's this? Poems? This kid writes poetry? What's our country coming to when a decent, well-bred kid who has a talent for forward passes and punts stoops to writing poetry?"

Hours later, the agents give up their search. As they climb out of the room (over stacks of albums, books and unwashed clothes) they fail to see (a) a switchblade, (b) a double-barreled shotgun, (c) an unmarked bottle of pills, (d) a bong . . . probably because they are prominently displayed on the top of the dresser.

You've got to hand it to these kids; they sure know how to hide things.

As for "shady transactions," all transactions conducted by kids are shady. The kids wouldn't have it any other way. It's not that the transactions are illegal, criminal, or even questionable; it's just that everything is more fun if Mom and Dad don't know about it.

The same goes for "clandestine affairs." As far as kids are concerned, those are the very best kind. And in many cases, they are the only kind.

From the day your child starts to school until the evening he drags a bunch of strangers to your wake, he'd rather you not know who his friends are. (Or to be more accurate, he'd rather his friends not know who you are.) Perhaps this is the parents' fault. When it comes to our children's friends, we tend to be nosy. We also tend to be snobs.

I recall one conversation we had years ago with one of our sons, who was then about sixteen years old. He had been out late the night before, and after interrogating him as to the whys and wheres, we finally got to the whos.

"Who were you out with?" I asked, after ascertaining that our son had been so late because he was driving and had to drop off six other kids.

"Just some guys," muttered our son.

"What guys?" I asked. "Don't they have names?"

"They're just some guys I go to school with. Don't sweat it, Mom; they're all good guys."

"I'm sure they are," I said, "but I'd just like to know who your friends are."

"Well, there was Sam Signatto and Heinie Rochman and Bill Ching and Lars Jorgenson and Chuck Juarez and Mike Anchokowvitz."

"Signatto . . . Ching . . . Juarez . . . Anchokowvitz . . . ye gods; don't you run around with any Americans?"

"Yeah," snapped our son. "Joe Running Water."

But sometimes the kids do carry their "clandestine" relationships to the extreme. I realized this not long ago when my husband looked up from the newspaper he was reading and said:

"Well, well. Guess who's engaged to be married?"

"Who?" I said. "And since when do you read the social news?"

"I don't usually, but the name caught my eye. It's Bloomingdale. It seems our son is getting married. Do we know a girl named Debbie?"

"Debbie? Of course! She's a darling girl! And she'll be a wonderful daughter-in-law! But I wonder why he didn't tell us! He knows how fond I am of Debbie!"

"Don't be ridiculous, Teresa," said my husband. "You know he couldn't bring himself to admit he's in love with a girl you like. Now, if you have any sense, you'll keep quiet about this; if you must mention it to him, frown when you do so. If you look the least bit happy about it, you're liable to blow the whole wedding."

Yes, indeed, I'm going to enjoy watching the CIA take on my children's generation; it should be quite a battle.

I only anticipate one problem. I won't know which side to root for.

23

The Intimidators

~~~~~~

*"Most mothers are the type of women who,
even when they aren't wearing a slip, are sure it is
showing."*

~~~~~~

"You look awful," my husband told me as he greeted me with
a kiss. "What's the matter? You're not sick, are you?"

"No," I assured him with a sigh. "I'm not sick. I'm just
exhausted and exasperated and frustrated and furious!"

"Let me guess," he said. "You have either been playing
bridge with What's-Her-Name, arguing with the plumber
again, or—and I shudder to suggest this—you just got home
from traffic court."

"Worse yet," I said. "I just got home from parent-teacher
conferences. I'm exhausted because I had to see six teachers
for each of our kids; I'm exasperated with some of the reports
and furious about others, and I'm frustrated because I can't
remember who said what about which child."

I hate parent-teacher conferences. I don't know why they
have them. The teachers detest them; the parents dread them,
and God knows the kids don't want them. So why have them?

I have been attending parent-teacher conferences since the first semester of Forever, and while I can count on my fingers the conferences where I was told that my child was doing well in class and was a joy to teach, the times I have been informed of missing assignments and skipped quizzes and classroom clowns who are "so bright, but they just won't study!" outnumber the hairs on my head.

Every semester I tell myself that I will forgo the "pleasure" of hearing these reports by somehow managing to "forget" the date of the conferences, but one or another of my kids will always manage to call it to my attention by saying something stupid like: "You can skip parent-teacher conferences this time because I'm doing just fine." This means, of course, that he is doing just awful, and I then feel obligated to attend the conferences if only to assure myself that he couldn't possibly be doing as bad as I suspect he might be. (He is.) Once at the conferences, I feel compelled to confer with my other children's teachers, as well as anyone else who has anything at all to do with my children, whether it be the principal on whose carpet they are so frequently called, the gym instructor who has an obsession about wearing gym shoes for gym, or the janitor who spends half his time erasing graffiti and sweeping up naughty notes and can never seem to remember who wrote any of them . . . until he sees me coming to the conferences.

At the last parent-teacher conference I received a total of twenty-four reports, some of them from teachers who had my children for one subject, some from teachers who had my children for two subjects, and one from a teacher who had two of my children for the same subject. I also conferred with four counselors, two janitors, and the principals of both the junior and senior high schools. By the time I limped home, I couldn't remember who was getting failing grades, who was up for the honors award, and who was supposed to stay after school every day next week to wash those words off the walls.

I know, I should take notes, but I am much too nervous to take notes. The truth is, teachers intimidate me. The teacher can be twenty-two years old, with a diploma so fresh it hasn't uncurled yet, still I approach her feeling guilty of crimes I had absolutely nothing to do with, unless mothering the criminals makes me an accessory before the fact.

I suppose a psychoanalyst would claim that my fear of teachers is a carryover from my convent-school days when the solemn-faced, black-habited nuns exerted such stern discipline. But that's not true. Those long-ago nuns never intimidated me, because I was Miss Goody-Two-Shoes, a fact which still rankles my prank-prone peers of yesteryear, and now that I think of it, makes me a little nauseous too.

No, the only nun who ever intimidated me was a sophisticated, slacks-clad feminist who let me overbid a bridge hand and then set me six no trump. And her being a nun had nothing to do with it; for that matter, neither did her being a feminist bother me. What intimidated me was her zeal as a bridge player.

I don't mind losing at bridge (which is a good thing, because I usually do), I just hate to play with people who take the game seriously. Bridge, to me, is not so much a game as an excuse to get together with my friends to gossip and go off my diet. If we squeeze a little cardplaying in between the gabbing and the gourmet dessert, that's okay, but not necessary. Everybody in my bridge foursome feels exactly the same way about this, so we get along famously.

However, occasionally we must get a substitute, and all too often it is the What's-Her-Name my husband referred to. She insists that we concentrate on the cards. I then play worse than ever, because no matter how hard I concentrate I can never remember who played what and certainly not who bid what. As I fumble my way along, the "sub" begins to sigh like a bored teenager forced to play Old Maid with her little sister, and if she is anxious to get the afternoon over with, so, most certainly, am I.

Last week our bridge foursome had to get a sub, and I was so relieved when What's-Her-Name couldn't come. But the sub we got was worse. She didn't sigh, or even roll her eyes, as my mother is wont to do when I trump my own trick. (Though I hasten to add that my mother never intimidates me, except sometimes on Sunday when she serves lemon meringue pie, which she makes from scratch.) This bridge player did not once comment on my mistakes. In fact, she did not comment on anything at all throughout the entire afternoon. The only time she spoke was to bid, in a self-confident, staccato-like tone, or to make such obvious announcements as: "You're down two; that's our game and rubber." We were all so intimidated by her we played the entire afternoon in almost total silence. It was awful. I got so nervous, it was all I could do to swallow a second helping of chocolate mousse.

Which leads me to yet another intimidator: the person who refuses to eat chocolate mousse, or any other dessert, because "I have to watch my figure, you know!" I don't know why she has to watch it; everybody else is watching it for her.

I have two friends who are near and dear to me, but they would be a lot dearer if they didn't look so darn good. They are both middle-aged mothers, with a total of ten children between them, yet they have managed to keep themselves so svelte they both have careers as professional models. Do you know what it does to my image to be seen with them? I'll tell you. It erases it. Because when I'm with them nobody sees me. It's true that neither of them has ever once criticized my figure, my clothes, or my coiffure, but I always have the feeling, when we get together, that they must shudder at the very sight of me.

I mentioned that fact at breakfast the other morning and my son said:

"Why should they shudder? I bet they love the way you look; it makes them look so much better!" (My son is a joy, but is somewhat lacking in tact. He once stopped his sister at a school dance and said: "I don't care what anybody says, Sis; I think you look terrific!" She didn't know whether to hug him or hit him.)

This same son too often subjects me to yet another form of intimidation: traffic court. Now, I have never in my life committed an offense requiring me to appear in traffic court, unless one counts, as one obviously must, bearing sons who cannot seem to remember the traffic laws. Having had numerous sons pass through the portals of traffic court, I have, over the years, become personally acquainted with every judge on the municipal court bench. Now, if there is anything more embarrassing than approaching a judge as a docket number, it is approaching a judge as an old friend. Somehow I would rather hear him say: "Case number 7777, are you the mother of this juvenile offender?" than "Hi, Teresa! Back again with the Road Runner, I see!" It doesn't make any difference that the judge is polite and courteous and friendly; I know what he is thinking: why doesn't that woman teach that kid to drive? It's doubly embarrassing, because I am the person who did teach that kid to drive . . . may God forgive me.

But if a judge intimidates me, it is nothing to the guilt I feel when I must confront my plumber. I call him "my" plumber because I have paid him so much over the years I feel I own him by now. I have been calling on the same plumber since my children were toddlers who, at the ages of two, three, four and five would spend half their time trying to flush their toys down the toilet, and the other half breaking the tank top, which they kept taking off to "see where everything goes when I flush." They also had a habit of jamming their toothbrushes down the bathroom sink drain (thus giving them an excuse not to brush their teeth), and on more than one occasion "cleaned" the fish bowl by dumping all its contents—water, fish, food and three cups of decorative sand—into the bathtub (which explains why the sewers in our neighborhood were sometimes so sluggish).

In those days, every time I called the plumber I initiated the conversation with an apology, as if I just knew he had more important things to do than work on people's pipes. When he arrived, I would apologize again, not only for the toy stuck in the toilet, but also for the condition of the bathroom, which, as any mother of any-age children can believe, was a perpetual mess. By the time the plumber and I were into the tenth year of our continuing relationship, I was not only apologizing for the behavior of my toddlers, but also for their very existence. It is true that the plumber never once commented on my delinquent children or their increasing number, but I knew what he was thinking; his very silence was a sermon on my incompetencies.

Eventually my children outgrew their bathroom capers, but they then moved up to more sophisticated stupidities, like dumping garbage into the kitchen sink. Like many kitchens, ours has a double sink, with a garbage disposal in one sink. Yet my kids invariably scrape the garbage into the other sink, absentmindedly washing it down the drain, where it settles stubbornly in the line until the plumber comes to retrieve it.

The kids claim it doesn't make any difference anyway, because the garbage disposal is so sensitive it won't eat anything but watered-down soup and maybe mashed potatoes, and they are probably right. I do know that my disposal jams so regularly my plumber now lists me as a "standing" in his appointment book.

I have long since stopped apologizing to the plumber for making him wealthy, and he has long since stopped his silent sermons. We have known each other for so long, he now feels free to criticize my plumbing procedures.

Just the other day I called him to unclog the disposal again, and as he was laboriously dismantling it, he grumbled: "How many times have I told you about celery hearts and banana peels? You can't put that kind of roughage in a garbage disposal!"

"I do not put banana peels or celery hearts in that disposal," I said huffily. "What do you think I am? An idiot?"

I know that my plumber and I are old friends as well as business associates, but he certainly didn't have to answer that question so promptly . . . or so literally.

24

Requiem
for a Sock-eater

~~~~~~

*"Children's socks are made in such a manner
that, when washed, one of each pair will either fade,
shrink or self-destruct."*

~~~~~~

"What's that?" asked my husband at breakfast one morning.
And he cocked an ear, as if to better hear some sound.

"What's what?" I asked.

"What's that I don't hear?" he asked. "Don't you not
hear it?"

"Are you all right?" I asked, wondering if perhaps he
had sneaked a bit of booze into his morning coffee.

"Listen!" he said. "There isn't any 'swish-plop-swish-
plop' noise in the laundry room. There is *always* a 'swish-
plop-swish-plop' noise in the laundry room! What do you suppose happened?"

"It must be the washing machine," I said, "or rather, it
must not be the washing machine . . . I mean it must be the
washing machine not going . . . what am I saying? . . . The
washing machine must be turned off!"

"Turned *off?*" asked my husband in mock astonishment. "I didn't know our washing machine had an 'off.' It's *always* on. It must be broken."

"It can't be broken!" cried our daughter Mary. "I have to wash my lingerie, and I have to be at work by noon. I certainly do not intend to go to work wearing no lingerie!" (And I am certainly glad to hear that!)

"Wash out your lingerie in the sink," I suggested. When I was your age, all our undergarments had to be hand-washed."

"Even the hoops?" quipped our son Dan.

"Watch your mouth, boy," I said. "If that machine is broken, it's probably your fault. Didn't I hear your gym shoes banging around in there last night? How many times have I told you not to wash your gym shoes in the washing machine?"

"It wasn't his gym shoes making all that noise," said his sister Peg; "it was his gym socks."

I went down to the laundry room and found our sixteen-year-old Ann frantically jiggling faucets and pushing buttons.

"Please don't be broken," she was begging the machine. "You can't quit now! Not in the middle of my new jeans! I haven't got anything else to wear!" (This is true. The fact that Ann's closet is full of clothes is irrelevant; those clothes have already been seen by her classmates, and obviously cannot be worn again unless we move out of the state.)

"Here, let me try," I said. I spent the next twenty minutes tightening faucets, cleaning out hoses, checking belts; I even changed the light bulb in the laundry-room ceiling. (I tried that last trick once before and it worked; the washing machine started right up. True, it could have been a coincidence, but in this household, who knows?) To my dismay, even that didn't work; the machine refused to go back on.

"I'll call the repairman," I said. "Just say a prayer this machine can be fixed; we can't afford a new one."

"It can't be fixed," said the heartless creature, who, after a single glance inside the machine, shook his head, picked up his never-opened toolbox, and handed me a bill for twenty-five dollars.

"Twenty-five dollars!" I exclaimed. "For what?"

"That's the minimum charge for a service call," he said.

"But you didn't *do* anything!" I said.

"I *came*," he said, truthfully, and I had to admit that he had not only come, but he had come promptly . . . the very day I had called him. But I do begrudge paying that kind of bill; it's rather like paying a surgeon when the patient died on the table. I realize the guy should be compensated for effort, but shouldn't there be a discount for failure?

"I'll tell you what I'll do," said the repairman cheerfully. "I'll haul it away for you free. I really am sorry I can't fix it, but this machine is dead!"

"What did it die from?" I asked. "Overwork?"

"Old age, I'd say," he mused. "I've been a washer repairman for ten years, and I've never even seen a model like that."

While the announcement that my washing machine was dead and about to be gone was shattering, it was not surprising, for it had lived long past a normal life-span. It had served me faithfully for seventeen years, working long, arduous hours, and I am quite sure that the only reason it didn't die long ago was because it knew how much I loved it.

How could you help but love something that has lived through so much with you? In its lifetime, that machine had washed thousands of diapers, hundreds of pairs of blue jeans, and millions and millions and millions of socks . . . of all sizes. It had worked its way up from baby buntings to basketball uniforms; it had seen me through bluebird uniforms, miniskirts, preppie clothes and college clothes, from short pants to blue jeans to chinos to polyester three-piece suits, and now, with the coming of our grandchildren, it was back to baby clothes. That's a lot of living for a washing machine. (That's a lot of living for a mother!)

I wasn't the only one who felt nostalgic about our washing machine. As the workman dismantled it to haul it away, our kids gathered round to reminisce.

"Just think," said Annie, fondly, "that washing machine is older than I am." Annie's affection was understandable. Since she turned into a clothes-conscious, fastidious teenager, Annie has spent more time in the laundry room than she has in the classroom.

"I remember the day we got it," said Mary with a sigh. "Mom was so excited; you would have thought we were getting a new car."

"I needed it more than a new car," I said. "As I recall, we had two babies in diapers then . . . washable diapers . . . and the old machine had been broken for almost a week. I was desperate! I think I had this machine going before the installer had even packed up his tools."

"And it's been going ever since," said Dan, whose bedroom is right over the laundry room.

"Gee, that machine *is* old," said Patrick, to whom everything over the age of five is "old." "If it could talk, just think of the stories it could tell!"

"Yeah," said Tim, "like the time it lived through the tornado! Remember when our house got destroyed by the tornado, and all our furniture got either broken or blown away? Then, a couple of days later, when the electricity finally came back on in the area, the neighbors heard a noise in our rubble, and it was the washing machine, finishing the cycle!"

"That's true," I said. "I had forgotten. And there was hardly a scratch on it; just that little dent in the side."

"Ah, yes, about that dent," said Dan, "there's something you might as well know about that dent, Mom, since the statute of limitations has run out. The tornado didn't make that dent; I did."

"You put that dent in the washing machine?" I asked. "When? Why? How?"

"It was the day before the tornado," said Dan. "Jim had left my new ten-speed out in the rain, and since it was *my* bike, Dad decided to punish *me;* he told me to clean the basement. I was so mad for being unjustly punished, I went downstairs and kicked the washing machine. Boy, was I glad to see that tornado; Dad would have killed me if he saw that dent!"

"Look!" I said, as the repairman turned the machine around before lifting it onto the lorry. "There's that mystery mural! We never did figure out how those gray paint splotches got on the side of the machine!"

"Is there a statute of limitations on lying?" asked Peg. "'Cause I lied about that, Mom, that day you lined us all up to grill us about those paint splotches."

"I remember that!" said Mary with a laugh. "Mom had lined us all up for the old third degree, and you insisted that since you were five years old you were old enough to be included in the lineup. You stood there at the end of the line, so proud of yourself, trembling right along with the rest of us. She never would have suspected you, Peg; you were nuts!"

"I was also guilty," said Peg, "but I had an accomplice! True, I was the one who picked the lock on Dad's workshop and climbed up and got the paint and brushes, but Annie did the actual painting."

"You mean you girls deliberately tried to paint the washing machine?" I asked. "But for heaven's sake, *why?* And why *gray,* of all colors?"

"Because you said you didn't like a plain old white washing machine," said Peggy. (Why is it that a girl who can't remember that it's her turn to do the dishes can recall the details of a prank she pulled twelve years ago?)

"I don't remember saying that," I said. "Why would I say something like that?"

"Because you were jealous of Aunt Madeleine," said Peg. "She had just bought a yellow washing machine and you said, 'Gee, it must be nice to have a color-coordinated laundry room.' So we decided to color-coordinate your laundry room, in 'basement gray,' only it was hard work and we didn't get it finished. Sorry about that."

"Sorry about what?" I asked, "That you painted the machine, or that you didn't get it finished?"

"Take your pick," said Peg cheerfully.

"Hey, where is everybody?" called our son Mike as he bounded down the basement stairs. "I just drove up from Lincoln; thought I might stay for dinner." (Sixty miles away, and he can smell a roast the minute I put it in the oven.)

"You're just in time," I said. "I've ordered a new washing machine; you and Dan can drive over to the Mart and pick it up."

"What's the matter with this one?" he asked. "Don't tell me you are going to get rid of it?"

"We have to," I said. "It can't be fixed."

At which point Michael fell upon the machine and began to rip the back off.

"What are you doing?" I cried. "I told you it can't be fixed!"

"I'm not trying to fix it," shouted Mike, "I'm going to rip its insides out!"

"But why?" I asked.

"To see what's in there!" he said. "My socks! My sweatbands! My class ring! My money! This monster's been eating my stuff for years! For all I know, it's still in here somewhere!"

Is it possible? Would my loyal, long-suffering, hardworking washing machine steal socks? And jewelry? And money? Impossible!

Anyway, it's not nice to think ill of the dead.

25

Call Me Grandma!

~~~~~~~~~~~~~~~~~~~~~~~~~~~~~~~~~~~~~~~

"If your baby is 'beautiful and perfect, never cries or fusses, sleeps on schedule and burps on demand, an angel all the time' . . . you're the grandma."

~~~~~~~~~~~~~~~~~~~~~~~~~~~~~~~~~~~~~~~

"I'm too young to be a grandmother!" I said as I paced the floor of my bedroom, watching the clock make its way toward midnight.

"Well, I'm too old to be a grandfather!" said my husband. "For cryin' out loud, will you come to bed and get some sleep! Lee will call you when the baby's born. Karen didn't even go to the hospital till three o'clock, and it's just a little after eleven. That's not long for a first labor. Quit worrying!"

"This is worse than having my own baby!" I said. "And it has been from the beginning. Who had the morning sickness when Karen got pregnant? I did. Who put on weight? I did." (A mother gets nervous, watching her daughter-in-law's diet.) "Who had the first labor pain? Lee did. And what mother wouldn't share her son's labor pains? I should have gone to the hospital with them. At least I could hold Lee's hand."

"No, you couldn't," said my husband sleepily. "He's holding Karen's hand. Have you forgotten, he's going to be with her throughout the whole thing! In fact, I think he intends to record it on film." (He did; we now have an R-rated scrapbook.)

I knew it would be silly for me to go to the hospital and walk the floor all by myself, so I stayed home and walked the living-room floor all by myself. The kids had called shortly before three o'clock to say that Karen had "had a few pains" and they were going to the hospital. They had not called since, but subsequent calls to their apartment had assured me that the pain was the real thing, and I was now waiting for the call that the baby had been born.

"It's been over eight hours!" I told my husband. "I'm going to call the hospital; something must have gone wrong!"

"Maternity!" said a sleepy voice in answer to my call.

"Is Karen Bloomingdale there?" I asked.

"Who?" asked the voice.

"Karen Bloomingdale," I repeated.

"Is she a nurse?" asked the voice.

"No, she's a patient! That is, she's a mother, or she's becoming a mother. I want to know how she is."

"She's not registered in maternity," said the voice, "but I think I remember seeing the name. Would you like me to ring Labor and Delivery?"

"Yes, please," I said impatiently.

"Labor and Delivery; can I help you?" Thank God, this voice wasn't so sleepy.

"I hope so," I said frantically. "Is Karen Bloomingdale in the labor room?"

"Karen Bloomingdale? Yeah, I think she is back there. Would you like me to check?"

"Oh, please!" I said.

A few moments later the voice returned.

"Nope; I was wrong. She's not there."

"Could she be in the delivery room?" I asked hopefully.

"Could be! I'll check!" How can she be so blasé at a time like this!

"I'm sorry," said another voice, this one much too professional, "Karen Bloomingdale is not in the delivery room."

"Then where is she?" I cried. "Has she already had her baby?"

"We cannot give out that information," said the voice. (I swear most hospital voices are recordings.)

"But you don't understand," I wailed. "I'm her mother-in-law, and they were supposed to keep me informed; I don't expect you to tell me if she had a boy or a girl or twins or even triplets. I just want to know if the baby has arrived and if everybody is all right! Surely, you can tell me; I'm the grandma!"

"I'm sorry," said the voice, "we cannot give out any information." Then a tiny relenting . . . "I can ring Recovery for you. Maybe somebody back there can help you." As I started to stutter my thanks, I heard the voice mutter in the background: "Hey, kid, you'd better get back to Recovery and answer the phone; it's your mom, and she's having a fit!"

"Hey, Mom! How ya' doin'?" said my son cheerfully when he answered the phone in Recovery. "Guess what? Karen just had a little boy! He's seven pounds fourteen ounces, and he looks just like me! How 'bout that!"

"Why didn't you call me!" I wailed. "I've been waiting for hours and hours! When was the baby born?"

"Approximately seven and a half minutes ago," he said. "You must have ESP! I just stepped out of the delivery room when a nurse told me you were calling. Wait'll you see this baby, Ma; what time will you and Dad come up in the morning?"

"In the morning?" I shouted. "Who's going to wait till

morning? We're coming up right now! I don't care how late it is; go down and see that the security guard lets us in! I'm not about to wait eight hours to see my grandson!"

I had forgotten how beautiful a newborn baby is. It is a myth that all babies look alike. Some newborn babies are red and scrawny and squally; others are pink and cuddly and cute. I suppose you think that, as a grandmother, I might be prejudiced about this particular baby, but my years as a journalist have made it possible for me to observe objectively, and in so doing, I have to admit that Joshua Lee Bloomingdale, at age fifty-three minutes, was the most beautiful baby God ever created.

My husband and I gloated and fawned over our grandson through the nursery glass until we were finally forced to bid him good night.

As we walked across the parking lot, the new grandpa sighed:

"I don't think I'm going to like this."

"You don't like being a grandfather?" I asked in surprise. "I thought you'd love the idea of having a child you could send home when he got naughty. Or is it the thought of being married to a grandmother that gets to you?"

"I'm thrilled to be a grandfather," he said, "and I will undoubtedly adjust to the idea of being married to a grandmother. What I can't bear is realizing that this baby is not ours."

"But he *is* ours!" I said. "He's our grandchild."

"I know, but he's not our *child*. We can't take him home! It will seem strange having him go home with Lee and Karen."

"It will seem strange having Lee and Karen go home!" I teased, recalling all the meals they just happened to drop by in time for. "Don't worry; you'll see plenty of this baby."

"I guess it's just that seeing all those new babies makes me want another one; I love new babies!"

"Since when?" I joked. "You were the one who always wished they could be born housebroken and able to play baseball! You had no patience at all with the squalling infants who leaked from both ends and spit up on every shirt you owned. It wasn't until they got into their terrible twos that you thought the kids were worth keeping!"

"That's not true and you know it," he said with a sigh. "I truly loved those infants, even the ones who couldn't tell time and kept us up all night. And you loved them too! Don't tell me you wouldn't just love to start all over again!"

"Okay, I won't tell you," I said. "But I'll tell the rest of the world. I DON'T WANT TO START ALL OVER AGAIN. True, I loved having a new baby every year . . . when I was young and lively and had not yet become addicted to sleep. But at our age? No, thank you. I'm too old to be a new mama!"

As we drove home, I began to wonder if I was perhaps even too old to be a grandma. It had been a long time since I had walked the floor with a colicky baby, and fought the battles of formula feeding and diaper rashes and runny noses. Yet I determined that I would be as helpful to my son and daughter-in-law as my own mother had been to me. When each of my babies were born, my mother came to spend a week with us; she got up at night with the baby; she taught me how to sterilize bottles, make formula, fold diapers (one way for boys, another for girls), bathe a squirming infant . . . I could not have survived that first week without her.

I knew I could never be the perfect grandma my mother was (and is!), but I was determined to try. I knew that the "other grandma," Karen's mother, lived a long distance away and had just started a new job; she could not possibly take off now to help her daughter. So . . . goody, goody! . . . I could get the job! I would teach Karen about sterilizers and formulas and double-soaking diapers. I would even be prepared to stay all night for the first few nights, till Karen got her strength back. I only hoped I was not too old for the task.

I soon found that I was not too old, but rather too young.

When my son complained that the baby was waking every two hours for middle-of-the-night feedings, I said:

"I've been expecting this; I'll tell you what I'll do. I will come every night for a week or so, and sleep in the nursery. That way I can get up with the baby and Karen can get her rest."

"Thanks for the offer, Mom," said my son, "but we've already got somebody to do that."

"You've already got somebody?" I asked in surprise. "You mean you hired a nurse? But that's ridiculous! Helping a new mother care for her baby is Grandma's job!"

"I know," he said with a smile. "That's whose helping."

"Lisa's here?" I asked, referring to Karen's mother. "I thought she couldn't come."

"She couldn't," said Lee, "but *her* mother could. You've met Karen's Grandma Brammer, haven't you? She's going to stay with us for a few days. Isn't that wonderful of her?"

"It certainly is," I said, finding it difficult to believe that the lovely white-haired lady I had met at their wedding was now a great-grandmother! "But you ought to be ashamed of yourself, imposing on a woman of her age!"

"I did hesitate to take her up on her offer," he admitted, "but not because of her age. It's her job I'm concerned about. But she assured us the nursing staff at the hospital could do without her for a few days." (Her job? Good Lord, doesn't anybody grow old anymore?) "It's really great, having somebody so capable helping with the baby."

"I'm sure it is," I pouted, and felt very incapable. "Well, I'm here if you need me!"

I needn't have pouted. Within days they needed me.

As anybody who has ever had a "first child" knows,

there is plenty of work to go around. I have yet to figure out why the first baby requires the constant attention of three grown women, while the second baby thrives on an occasional hug from a preoccupied parent. It wasn't long before my grandson was deposited on my doorstep with a plea from his parents:

"Could you take care of Josh for the evening? We've got to get some time to ourselves!"

"Did we ever get any time to ourselves?" I asked my husband as we happily unwrapped the layers of blanket enfolding our perfect grandson.

"We must have," he said. "Otherwise we never would have had the other nine. Do you need some help?"

"As a matter of fact, I do," I said. "The baby needs to be changed, and I can't find his diapers. Karen said they were in this bag, but I can't find anything in here but these things . . ."

"Those 'things' are Pampers, Teresa," said my husband. "Haven't you ever seen a disposable diaper before?"

"Listen, for a fellow who fathered five babies before he ever touched *any* diapers, you have a lot of gall laughing at me. Where would I ever see a disposable diaper?"

"On television, of course," he said. "How could you miss all those baby commercials?"

"I miss all the commercials I can," I admitted. "Okay, this does begin to look like a diaper; now, if I can just figure out how to fold it . . ."

"It's prefolded, Teresa," said the Expert. "They're made that way."

"What a clever idea!" I said. "I wonder why Birds Eye never thought of that?"

"They probably did, in later years, but by that time we were all through with diapers. What's the matter now?"

"I can't find the pins," I said. "You took the baby's diaper off; where did you put the pins?"

"What pins?" he asked. "There weren't any pins."

"There had to be pins!" I said, searching frantically beneath the baby. "How do you think he kept his diaper on?"

"Simple," said Mr. Know Everything. "See the little tabs? They're adhesive; you just glue the diaper on. Here, let me show you."

"Forget it now," I said. "It's too late; the baby needs to be changed again."

"You can't," said my husband.

"Yes, I can," I said. "I've got it figured out now . . ."

"No, I mean you can't change him yet; Lee said he can only be changed twice every hour."

"Why just twice?" I asked.

"Because that's all their budget can afford," he said. "At twelve cents a diaper, even twice an hour could run over five dollars a day!"

"I just remembered something," I said. "Watch the baby a minute; I'll be right back."

I went upstairs and rummaged through the storage closet, found what I was looking for, and went back to find my husband bouncing one very damp baby on his knee.

"Here," I said. "We'll put this on the baby."

"What is it?" he asked.

"What does it look like? It's a diaper. A real one. I just remembered that I bought a dozen gauze diapers at the white sale last January."

"Anticipating the new grandchild?" he asked.

"No," I admitted, "anticipating spring housecleaning. I don't know what modern mothers use for rags; personally, I've never learned to use anything but diapers."

"But what about diaper pins?" he asked.

"I have some right here," I said, producing a rather worn pair of baby-blue bunny-head safety pins.

"Where on earth did you find those?" he asked in astonishment.

"In my bathrobe pocket," I admitted.

"You're kidding!" He laughed. "Are you sentimental . . . or just sloppy?"

"Neither," I admitted. "Just frugal. I thought I might need these someday."

Well, how was I to know that diaper pins would become as passé as diaper pails?

While the baby took his nap, I went to the basement and sadly disposed of all those other "frugalities" I had planned on using someday: the sterilizer (no longer needed in this era of disposable bottles), the glass nursing bottles, the old faithful (if somewhat unsturdy) playpen, the never-certified-for-safety car seat, the teetering high chair. I felt as outdated as all of them. What did I know of modern baby care, with their canned formula and paper diapers and combination car-seat/jump-seat/feeding-chair? My grandson would have the latest-model stroller, swing set, high chair, crib. What need had he of an "old model" mother like me?

And then I saw it, in the corner of the basement. Dusty, nicked and scratched by ten little toddlers who had once used it for a car, a spaceship, a sailing vessel, a train. How many wonderful hours had my babies and I spent in Grandma's rocker?

I dragged it upstairs, dusted it off, and placed it in the corner of the living room. The moment my grandson began to fuss, I gently lifted him from his crib and, cuddling him on my lap, began to sing: "Lullaby, and good night, with roses bedight . . ." I sang the old familiar lullabies; I hummed the old familiar hymns, and I felt the old familiar love, and awe, and peace that only a parent can know . . . and only a grandparent can appreciate.

I think, after all, I may be just the right age to be a grandma.

About the Author

TERESA BLOOMINGDALE's humor and wit have made her two previous books, *I Should Have Seen It Coming When the Rabbit Died* and *Up a Family Tree,* big successes and have won her many fans from across the country. In addition to writing a weekly newspaper column, she has had articles published in such leading magazines as *Good Housekeeping* and *McCall's,* for which she is a contributing editor. Her other books, which were selected by the Doubleday Book Club and the Literary Guild, have also been excerpted in dozens of newspapers nationwide. When not at home in Omaha, Nebraska, with attorney-husband A. Lee Bloomingdale and seven of their ten children, she can be found on the lecture circuit, where she is in popular demand.